THE CRIME WRITER'S
HANDBOOK

Other Allison & Busby Writers' Guides

How to Write Stories for Magazines by Donna Baker
How to Write Five-Minute Features by Alison Chisholm
A Practical Poetry Course by Alison Chisholm
The Craft of Writing Poetry by Alison Chisholm
How to Write for the Religious Markets by Brenda Courtie
How to Produce a Play by Doris M. Day
The Craft of Novel-Writing by Dianne Doubtfire
Writing for Radio by Colin Haydn Evans
How to Publish Your Poetry by Peter Finch
How to Publish Yourself by Peter Finch
How to Write a Play by Dilys Gater
The Craft of TV Copywriting by John Harding
How to Write A Blockbuster by Sarah Harrison
How to Write for Children by Tessa Krailing
How to Write Crime Novels by Isobel Lambot
The Craft of Food and Cookery Writing by Janet Laurence
Dear Author . . . by Michael Legat
How to Write Historical Novels by Michael Legat
Writing Step by Step by Jean Saunders
The Craft of Writing Romance by Jean Saunders
How to Create Fictional Characters by Jean Saunders
How to Research Your Novel by Jean Saunders
How to Write Realistic Dialogue by Jean Saunders
How to Write Advertising Features by John Paxton Sheriff
The Craft of Writing TV Comedy by Lew Schwarz
How to Write Science Fiction by Bob Shaw
How to Write and Sell Travel Articles by Cathy Smith
How to Compile and Sell Crosswords and Other Puzzles
    by Graham R Stevenson
The Craft of Writing Articles by Gordon Wells
The Magazine Writer's Handbook 1997/8 by Gordon Wells
The Book Writer's Handbook 1996/7 by Gordon Wells
How to Write Non-Fiction Books by Gordon Wells
Writers' Questions Answered by Gordon Wells
Photography for Article-Writers by Gordon Wells
The Best of Writers' Monthly by Gordon Wells
How to Write and Sell a Synopsis by Stella Whitelaw
How to Write for Teenagers by David Silwyn Williams
How to Write and Sell Interviews by Sally-Jayne Wright

THE CRIME WRITER'S HANDBOOK

First Edition

Douglas Wynn

a&b

First published in Great Britain in 1997 by
Allison & Busby Ltd
114 New Cavendish Street
London W1M 7FD
http://www.allisonandbusby.ltd.uk

Reprinted 1998

A catalogue record for this book is available from
the British Library.

ISBN 0 7490 0345 6

Designed and typeset by N-J Design Associates
Romsey, Hampshire
Printed and bound in Great Britain by
WBC Book Manufacturers
Bridgend, Mid Glamorgan

CONTENTS

1   **Introduction to The Crime Writer's Handbook**   1

2. **Methods of Murder – Introduction**   3
       Accidents (Contrived)   4
       Animals: Attack by a trained animal   5
       Animals: Poisonous fish   6
       Animals: Poisonous jellyfish and octopuses   7
       Animals: Poisonous snakes I   8
       Animals: Poisonous snakes II   9
       Animals: Poisonous spiders and scorpions   10
       Asphyxia   11
       Automatism   12
       Axe   13
       Bacterial poisoning   14
       Blunt instrument   15
       Burning   16
       Crossbows   17
       Defenestration   18
       Disposal of the body I   19
       Disposal of the body II   20
       Drowning   21
       Electrocution   22
       Embolism (Air)   23
       Explosives   24
       Firearms (Smooth bore)   25
       Firearms (Rifled) Handguns   26
       Firearms (Rifled) Rifles and machine pistols   27
       Hanging   28
       Hit-and-run   29
       Impossibilities and miscellaneous methods   30
       Karate   31
       Kidnapping   32
       Masochism   33
       Poisons (Introduction)   34
       Poisons (Legal aspects)   35
       Poisons from fungi   36
       Poisons from plants: Aconite   37
       Poisons from plants: Belladonna   38

Poisons from plants: Curare   39
Poisons from plants: Digitalis   40
Poisons from plants: Hemlock   41
Poisons from plants: Hyoscine   42
Poisons from plants: Ricin   43
Poisons from plants: Strychnine   44
Poisons (Industrial) Antimony   45
Poisons (Industrial) Arsenic   46
Poisons (Industrial) Carbon monoxide   47
Poisons (Industrial) Cyanide   48
Poisons (Industrial) Mercury   49
Poisons (Industrial) Phosphorus   50
Poisons (Industrial) Thallium   51
Poisons (Medical) Cantharidin   52
Poisons (Medical) Chloroform   53
Poisons (Medical) Insulin   54
Poisons (Medical) Morphine and codeine   55
Poisons (Medical) Sleeping pills I   56
Poisons (Medical) Sleeping pills II   57
Poisons (Pesticides) Nicotine   58
Poisons (Pesticides) Paraquat   59
Poisons (Pesticides) Parathion   60
Poisons (Street drugs) Amphetamines   61
Poisons (Street drugs) Cocaine   62
Poisons (Street drugs) Heroin   63
Sharp instruments   64
Strangulation   65
Suffocation   66
Throat-cutting   67

3. Methods of Detection and Forensic Science –   68
   Introduction
Adipocere   69
Ballistics   70
Bite-mark analysis   71
Blood (Bloodstains)   72
Blood (Serology)   73
Bruises   74
Cadaveric spasm   75
Computers   76
Contact traces   77
Crime kits   78
Decomposition (Putrefaction)   79

DNA profiling 80
Exhumation 81
Facial reconstruction 82
Fibres 83
Fingerprints 84
Forensic entomology 85
Forensic odontology 86
Forensic psychiatry 87
Forensic psychology (Psychological profiling) 88
Glove prints 89
Gunshot wounds 90
Hair 91
Head wounds 92
Hypnosis 93
Identification (Identity parades) 94
Identification (Identikit, photo-fit, etc.) 95
Knife wounds 96
Lividity 97
Mummification 98
Paint or varnish 99
Palm prints, footprints etc. 100
Polygraph 101
Post-mortem (Autopsy) I 102
Post-mortem Procedure II 103
Psychic detection 104
Rigor mortis 105
Scenes of crime procedures 106
Schizophrenia 107
Semen 108
Sex crimes 109
Sex crimes (Investigation) 110
Skeletons 111
Skulls 112
Stomach contents 113
Time of death 114
Voice prints 115

4   Other Aspects of Crime – Introduction 116
Child murder 117
Confessions 118
Conspiracy to murder 119
Coroner 120
Corpus delicti 121

Crime passionel   122
Evidence   123
Evidence (Circumstantial)   124
Folie à deux   125
Homicide   126
Infanticide   127
Interpol   128
Jury system   129
Manslaughter   130
Multiple murder (Mass and spree killers)   131
Multiple murder (Serial killers)   132
Murder   133
Police procedure (Force structure)   134
Police procedure (Mechanics of a murder investigation)   135
Police procedure (Arrest and interview)   136
Reasonable doubt   137

Appendix   138

Bibliography   139

ACKNOWLEDGEMENTS

My most sincere thanks must go to Gordon Wells, without whom this book would never have been written. He had the original idea, suggested much of the format and acted as a kind of literary midwife for the project. I should also like to thank Martin Edwards for allowing me to use his encyclopaedic knowledge of crime fiction and giving me a preview of his contribution to the *Oxford Companion To Crime & Mystery Writing* (St. James Press, 1997). I am grateful to David Acaster and Roger Forsdyke, both serving policemen, for sharing their deep knowledge of police matters with me. Thanks are also due to Dr Susan M. Pringle, who sent literature from the dayschool, the Science of Crime Detection, which she runs at the University of Bristol. And to the many experts who answered my questions and gave me information, I record my indebtedness. But I should emphasise that, if there are any mistakes in the book, they are mine, and mine alone.

Lastly, but most importantly, thanks to my wife Rosemary, for her continuing help and encouragement.

CHAPTER 1

INTRODUCTION TO THE CRIME WRITER'S HANDBOOK

The other day I was talking to a serving policeman, who is also a devotee of crime fiction, and he said that he was astonished at the lack of elementary knowledge of police procedure in a book he had been reading by an established novelist. It quite spoilt the book for him. But he was offended because he was a policeman. The book might not have worried anyone else who hadn't his specialised knowledge. How much this matters is obviously partly the personal decision of the writer. If you want your book to be as factually accurate as it is possible to be then it matters a great deal. If you don't – perhaps you feel your book is much more a work of imagination – then you might not mind if it has technical inaccuracies. But the reading public is becoming more technically aware. Television science programmes tell us about DNA, or the latest medical breakthrough and what is happening in space. And there are many more popular science books about than there used to be. In the same way, television is awash with police programmes. People are exposed to much more technical information that they ever used to be. And I think crime writers ignore this at their peril.

So this encyclopaedia is an attempt to redress the balance, to provide crime-writers with something they can dip into and, hopefully, find useful information. I have tried to cover as wide as field as possible. But in a book as short as this there must obviously be some restrictions. The decision as to what to put in is mine and if I have missed anything out I apologise in advance.

Another object of the book is the sparking of creativity. Writers are always looking for ideas and I hope that reading about various aspects of crime will help with plots, ideas for methods of murder, components of the investigation and so on.

After this introduction, the book is divided into three sections: Methods of Murder; Methods of Detection and Forensic Science; and a miscellaneous section including police procedure, the legal system and so on. In each of the sections the entries are in alphabetical order and the sub-division of the entries, the summary box at the top of the page and the use of real life and fictional examples are explained in the appropriate introduction to each section.

The bibliography only includes non-fiction books. Where I have given fiction examples in the text I have also quoted the author and the name

1

of the novel. You should also remember that real-life examples can be researched from national or local newspapers, which can often be obtained from your local library. If not, I can recommend a trip to the British Library, Newspaper Library, Colindale Avenue, London NW5 5HE, telephone 0171 323 7353.

CHAPTER 2

METHODS OF MURDER – INTRODUCTION

In this chapter, I list methods of murder alphabetically. I have also cross-referenced other methods, and entries in other chapters, by putting the words which form the headings in capital letters. At the top right-hand side of each entry in this chapter I have put a summary box giving a quick estimate of what I judge will be the relative usefulness of the method to crime-fiction writers. I have scored the categories in marks out of ten to indicate the relative Availability of the method to a potential murderer, the Effectiveness in terms of the quick and less messy kill and how easy the method would be to detect by an investigator – its Detectability. A high score indicates an easy method to detect. This section is particularly important for poisons, but may not be so obviously important for some other methods.

Each entry begins with an introduction and description of the method, followed by a separate section on its effects, usually on the body. Of necessity it is a little gruesome and may be a trifle clinical, though I have tried to keep technical terms to the minimum. But it is important for writers to know the detailed effects of many murder methods even if they decide not to record the details in their books. It would be better, for example, not to have the victims thrashing about in agony if in reality they would be comatose!

I have included a section on examples of the use of the method in real life and given names, dates and places so that readers can research the case if they wish. In my opinion there are few better ways of establishing believable characters in fiction than by discovering the motives and characters of real people and the way they go about things. And one can do this by reading accounts of actual crimes and how they were solved.

The sections on fictional examples are much less detailed because I think it is unfair to the author, especially in whodunits, to give away too much of the story. So I have given only the briefest details, simply to indicate which method was used.

2 ACCIDENTS (CONTRIVED)

Availability	(1)8/10 (2)9/10 (3)7/10 (4)6/10
Effectiveness	(1)5/10 (2)6/10 (3)7/10 (4)8/10
Detectability	(1)2/10 (2)8/10 (3)6/10 (4)5/10

1. Falls – This is a common fictional contrived accident, but its effectiveness in reality is chancy. A 'controlled fall', that is, one where you land upright, is survivable from up to 100 feet. But an 'uncontrolled fall', where other parts of the body hit the ground first, can be lethal in a much shorter distance. Falling off a step-ladder can kill you if you land on your head.

2. Arson – setting fire to buildings and vehicles has been used in real life to murder people. Pushing burning material through the letter-box of a house is an easy way to start a fire, but firing buildings may not be all that effective in killing people and it is difficult to make an arson attack look like an accidental fire.

3. Motor vehicles – can be quite effective if the victim is hit at high speed by a vehicle or the vehicle driven over a cliff, but the certainty of doing either may not be all that high. And running over an unconscious victim to make it look like a street accident is easily detected by forensic experts.

4. Machinery – a wide range of possibilities exists here, from industrial machinery to farm implements. Electrical equipment is covered elsewhere (*see* ELECTROCUTION page 22). Among other things, victims can fall into vats of fermented brews or various noxious chemical liquids. A certain amount of technical knowledge is required and a suitable location, such as a factory or brewery.

REAL-LIFE EXAMPLES
- Virginia McGinnis was convicted of the murder of young Deana Wild, by pushing her off a cliff at Big Sur, California, in April, 1987, saying that the girl slipped in her high heels, and then trying to claim the insurance.
- Alfred Rouse combined arson and cars. To get out of a difficult situation he had got himself into with several women, he tried to fake his death by setting fire to his car (with an unknown passenger he had picked up still inside it). He tried to make it look like an accident, but was convicted of murder in January, 1931.

FICTIONAL EXAMPLES
- Sheila Radley has a character run over and killed in a contrived accident in *Who Saw Him Die?*
- A body is found in a tank of liquid clay in *The Spoilt Kill* by Mary Kelly.
- Death by a heavy object falling on a victim has appeared in several books. Agatha Christie uses this method in *Murder in Mesopotamia* and *Nemesis*.

2. ANIMALS: ATTACK BY A TRAINED ANIMAL

Availability	6/10
Effectiveness	5/10
Detectability	6/10

Murder by an animal is not unknown in fiction, but very rare in real life. Unless simply placing the victim near the animal will result in a fatal assault, as in the case of a POISONOUS SNAKE (*see* page 8, 9), the animal must be trained to attack. With dogs, this is not as difficult as it might seem. They are pack animals and by instinct will follow the commands of the leader. The human who owns the animal, or the person who feeds and trains it, can become the pack leader. And some very aggressive breeds, such as those used for guard duties, can be trained to attack people – even the trainer's own family – on a given command. This is well illustrated in the case which follows.

REAL-LIFE EXAMPLES

● In September, 1992, police were called to a house in Cleveland, Ohio, where they found a dead young woman, Angela Kaplan, with severe dog-bites to her arms. She had died from loss of blood. Her boyfriend, Jeffrey Mann, with whom she lived, said she had been attacked by a strange dog. But he himself had a five-stone pit-bull terrier in the house. The police found plenty of evidence that the dog had been very friendly towards Angela. There was even a photograph showing the animal lying contentedly in the young woman's arms. But dog experts were able to show that the dog had been trained to attack. And the prosecution, at Jeffrey Mann's trial for murder, declared that the dog must have been repeatedly commanded to attack since Angela had 180 separate bites to her arms. The evidence of the experts convinced the jury that the onslaught was planned and instigated by Mann, rather than being a random assault by the pit-bull. Jeffrey was convicted of murder and, because the experts could not discover what the command to attack had been and thus couldn't risk the animal attacking anyone else, the pit-bull was put down.

FICTIONAL EXAMPLES

● A trained ape kills two women albeit by accident, in *Murders in The Rue Morgue,* by Edgar Allan Poe.
● A large dog is responsible for several deaths in Conan Doyle's *The Hound Of The Baskervilles*.

2 ANIMALS: POISONOUS FISH

Availability	4/10
Effectiveness	6/10
Detectability	3/10

There are two kinds of poisonous fish: those that are poisonous to touch and those that are poisonous to eat. Of the first, the scorpionfish, the zebrafish and the stonefish are the most well known. The scorpionfish is found in the warmer parts of the Pacific Ocean, the zebrafish in the Red Sea and Indian Ocean and the stonefish around China, the Philippines and Australia. But varieties of all three can be found in aquariums; the most familiar stonefish species in captivity being among the most venomous.

They are usually about four to eight inches long and live in shallow waters, hiding in coral caves or buried in the sand or mud so that an unwary swimmer can easily step on one. Their spines, which they erect at the first signs of disturbance, are extremely poisonous.

EFFECTS
- Instantaneous intense pain and swelling near the site of the sting, followed by convulsions, paralysis and unconsciousness leading eventually to cardiac arrest. Stonefish antivenin is available but may not be easy to obtain quickly.

Of the fish which are poisonous to eat, probably the most common is the Pufferfish, so-called because it puffs itself up when frightened. It is found in warm or temperate seas around the world and is a revered delicacy in Japan, where it is called *fugu*. The toxic parts are the liver, ovaries and the roe, which contain tetrodotoxin, an extremely poisonous and difficult-to-detect substance. But, if the entrails of the fish are removed carefully, the flesh of the fish can be safely eaten. However, there are over a hundred deaths recorded every year in Japan due to eating pufferfish.

EFFECTS
- Paralysis sets in within ten minutes, but can be delayed for up to four hours. The victim has difficulty speaking and this rapidly progresses to respiratory paralysis, convulsions and death within one to two hours.

REAL-LIFE EXAMPLES
- In 1774, natives tried to poison the explorer Captain James Cook by giving him pufferfish. There is also some evidence that this drug has been used in Haiti in the zombie rituals.

FICTIONAL EXAMPLES
- Tetrodotoxin was used in the film *The Serpent and the Rainbow* to slow the respiration and make a victim look as if he was dead. He was buried, but quickly dug up and continued small doses of poison made him a zombie or one of the 'living dead'.

2 ANIMALS: POISONOUS JELLYFISH AND OCTOPUSES

Availability   3/10
Effectiveness   7/10
Detectability   3/10

There are over 200 species of jellyfish. The translucent, sometimes coloured, gelatinous body is bell- or umbrella-shaped with a central tubular projection that hangs down in the middle and contains the mouth. Around the outside, dangle four or more tentacles which are usually sticky and contain stinging capsules within the threads. Jellyfish occur in all oceans but are more common in the tropics.

EFFECTS
● The dangerous varieties, like the sea wasp (found off beaches in Queensland, Australia), and the Portuguese man-of-war (in European waters), give stings which can be mildly irritating or sometimes lethal if the victim is a child or has a weak heart. In severe cases, chest and abdominal pain is experienced, with difficulty in swallowing, which leads to respiratory and cardiac depression. For swimmers, out of reach of land, however, an attack can lead to drowning. Victims are often covered in sticky threads and weals arise where stinging has taken place, which may leave permanent scars.

REAL-LIFE EXAMPLES
● In January 1955, a five-year-old boy was stung by jellyfish in only two feet of water on a Queensland beach. He collapsed and died in two minutes.

Octopuses are found in most oceans and only a few are dangerous to man. The blue-ringed octopus (which is found off the coast of North America) and the Australian spotted octopus are both small, about six inches across. Normally they are harmless unless handled, but can then give stings which are not noticed until the symptoms of poisoning begin.

EFFECTS
● The venom affects the central nervous system leading to paralysis of the muscles so that breathing eventually stops and the victim dies. But it takes some time before full paralysis is reached and administration of oxygen in hospital may save the patient. During swimming, a victim is unlikely to survive.

REAL-LIFE EXAMPLES
● In 1967, a young soldier playing with a small octopus on a beach noticed some blood on his hand when he put the creature down. He felt a numb sensation round his mouth. Fifteen minutes later, he was severely paralysed and hardly able to breath. He was rushed to hospital, put on a heart-lung machine and, eventually, survived.

7

2 ANIMALS: POISONOUS SNAKES I

Availability	5/10
Effectiveness	6/10
Detectability	8/10

The venom of poisonous snakes is lethal – but it does not make a good method of murder. For a full-grown person, a snake bite is rarely fatal because a snake does not use all its venom in one strike. For maximum effect, the venom also needs to reach the bloodstream, so unless a vein or artery is punctured by the bite the effect is not so great. In addition, antidotes to many snake venoms are available and if the type of snake can be identified and the antivenom administered quickly the victim will recover. On the other hand, if snake venom is injected into the bloodstream or enters by means of a cut it will then have the maximum effect. All snake venoms are complex proteins which affect the sensory and motor nerves and those of the heart and lungs.

Rattlesnake
● Found in most arid regions from Canada to South America, rattlesnake venom causes excessive thirst, nausea, vomiting and paralysis. Death occurs usually because of kidney failure, but is rare in populated regions because of the availability of antivenom. Reaction times vary between fifteen minutes and two hours.

Cottonmouth
● So called because it threatens with its mouth open, showing its white interior. It is found in swampy and wooded regions mainly in the Eastern USA. The venom literally dissolves tissue and the site of the bite eventually becomes gangrenous. Haemorrhages occur in the heart and lungs and the victim appears to bleed to death. Effects begin almost immediately, but antivenom is held in most American hospitals.

REAL-LIFE EXAMPLES
● Robert James, who lived in Los Angeles in 1936, insured his wife for a substantial amount of money – then strapped her to the kitchen table and thrust her bare foot into a box containing two rattlesnakes. She was bitten, but, though her foot and leg swelled alarmingly and she was in great pain, she did not die. So James drowned her in the bath and then took her body out to the garden pond to make it look as if she had tripped and fallen in. But he had involved a friend in the murder, who soon talked and James was hanged in 1942, the last person to be executed by this means in California.

2 ANIMALS: POISONOUS SNAKES II

Availability	3/10
Effectiveness	8/10
Detectability	5/10

Cobra Family

● Cobras are found in many hot parts of the world, from Africa to Asia and on to the Americas. They are part of the viper family and some of them can expand their neck ribs to form a hood. The king cobra is the biggest, growing from 12 to 18 feet long and is the world's largest venomous snake, although its venom is not all that toxic, being lethal in only about ten per cent of cases.

● The Egyptian or Asian cobra, better known as Cleopatra's asp, can grow to six feet in length.

● The black-necked cobra is very aggressive and can spit venom into a victim's eyes from seven feet away. And, while the venom does not harm the flesh, it can cause blindness if the eyes are not washed quickly.

● Cobras which do not have a hood include the black mamba (which is actually grey or greenish brown). It can grow to 14 feet, often hunts in trees, and is extremely aggressive. It can rear up six feet or more to inflict a bite, which is 100 per cent lethal unless antivenom is given quickly.

● The taipan is Australia's largest cobra, growing to nearly 11 feet and is also a very aggressive snake, inflicting many bites when it attacks. Its venom contains a blood-clotting agent which can be fatal within minutes.

EFFECTS

● Cobra venom contains powerful neurotoxins which lead to paralysis of the muscles. Death occurs by respiratory failure. Symptoms start after 15 to 30 minutes and involve pain, swelling of the affected limb, convulsions and a fall in blood pressure. The site of the injury is not markedly affected, as it is with some snake bites, and usually no gross abnormalities of internal organs are seen on post-mortem. For recovery from the more toxic venoms, administration of the specific antivenom must be given quickly or death will occur within two hours. Most cobra venoms are twice as toxic as STRYCHNINE (*see* page 44), five times as lethal as that from the black widow spider (*see* POISONOUS SPIDERS page 10), but only half as potent as the mushroom poison amanitine (*see* POISONS FROM FUNGI page 36).

REAL-LIFE EXAMPLES

● There have been quite a few suicides using poisonous snakes. Cleopatra's is probably the most famous. Cleopatra was alleged to be Julius Caesar's lover and was certainly Antony's. After being defeated at Actium by Octavian in 30BC, Antony and Cleopatra committed suicide.

● More recently, an American bacteriologist injected himself with cobra venom and died within a few minutes.

2 ANIMALS: POISONOUS SPIDERS AND SCORPIONS

Availability	4/10
Effectiveness	6/10
Detectability	5/10

Spiders
- The most dangerous thing about poisonous-spider bites is not their toxicity, which is usually less than that of POISONOUS SNAKES (*see* pages 8 and 9), but the fact that the bite is not often felt and the victim does not realise that anything is wrong until the symptoms begin.
- The brown recluse, or fiddle-back spider, is one of the most dangerous. Found in the southern states of the USA, its bite is usually painless and symptoms take from two to eight hours to develop. Pain is followed by blisters and ulceration of the bite area and the victim may suffer flu-like symptoms. The toxin is rarely fatal unless untreated but death may occur due to renal failure.
- The black widow spider is even better-known and is found all over the world in warm climates. Unlike the brown recluse, this spider often resides in houses and sometimes under toilet seats. Bites in the genital area are not uncommon. Again its bite is almost painless and flu-like symptoms develop later. But – belying its fearsome reputation – its toxin is even less potent than the brown recluse.

Scorpions
- These creatures prefer hot, arid regions and are found all over the world. They are not aggressive, however, and very few species have venom strong enough to kill a human being. Only one in a thousand stings is fatal, due to the fact that a single sting releases very little venom. If it could be collected and injected into the blood stream, it would be much more effective. The more deadly types are the common striped scorpion, the brown scorpion, devil scorpion and the giant hairy scorpion.
- The venom of scorpions contains neurotoxins which can lead to respiratory failure and, as with poisonous spiders, the sting of the more dangerous ones is not as painful as those from the less dangerous. Muscular spasms and stomach cramps may occur within two to four hours and go on for 24 to 48 hours. But antisera are available for most scorpion stings and applying a tourniquet above the site of the wound, where this is possible, often limits the absorption.

2 ASPHYXIA

Availability 8/10
Effectiveness 6/10
Detectability 8/10

Reducing or cutting off air or oxygen to the lungs results in a condition known as asphyxia. Medically speaking, any process which interferes with the oxygen-carrying capacity of the blood, such as ELECTROCU-TION (*see* page 22), AIR EMBOLISM (*see* page 23), or various poisons, can be classed as asphyxiation. This includes STRANGULATION (*see* page 65); SUFFOCATION (*see* page 66); HANGING (*see* page 28); over-laying – where a person smothers a baby by lying on it (usually accidentally) or with a pillow; and crush asphyxia, where the chest wall is compressed.

EFFECTS
- For all manual asphyxiations there are three characteristic stages. First there is an increase in pulse rate and rise in blood pressure as the victim gasps and struggles for breath. Then, the face becomes congested, cyanosis (blueness of the skin) develops, and the eyes begin to bulge as consciousness starts disappearing. Finally, convulsions may take place and breathing becomes very shallow. Unconsciousness is complete and muscles twitch as death occurs.
- Death can take as long as five minutes. The vagus nerve, however, which controls the slowing-down of the heart, runs alongside the jugular vein in the neck. Compression of the neck can sometimes cause stimulation of the nerve and the heart may stop quickly before asphyxiation has run its normal course. This is called vagal inhibition.
- Detection is usually relatively easy. Finger marks can often be seen on the neck as bruises, and marks of a ligature can be similarly observed. The lips and ears go bluish and the same colour stains the fingernails. There may be froth and blood-staining around the nose and mouth. The tongue is forced outwards and the hands clenched. And burst blood capillaries (*petechiae*) can be seen in the heart, lungs and in the eyes.

REAL-LIFE EXAMPLES
- In the 1820s Burke and Hare gave rise to a new word. These two Irish labourers used to supply corpses for anatomical dissection at Edinburgh's medical school. They would lure a vagrant back to their lodgings and, when he or she became insensible through drink, sit on their chests while covering the mouth and nostrils with a blanket, until they were asphyxiated. The technique became known as 'burking'.

2 AUTOMATISM

Availability 2/10
Effectiveness 8/10
Detectability 5/10

Automatic behaviour, where people are unaware of what they are doing and often cannot remember afterwards what they have done, is recognised in law as being one of two states: 'insane and non-insane automatism'. The latter is the defence of sleepwalking and, though there have been some notable instances where murder-case juries have accepted such a defence, it is very difficult to sustain, particularly in Britain.

The commonest cause of insane automatism is epilepsy. After a major epileptic fit (*grand mal*) the patient may enter a state of epileptic automatism where their actions are irrational and they later have little memory of what they have done. The defence is that the patient was not responsible for his actions. Psychomotor epilepsy is another and very rare form of the disorder in which the patient is apparently normal, but suffers personality instability and lack of emotional control. Psychiatrists supporting the defence of Jack Ruby for shooting Lee Harvey Oswald claimed Ruby was suffering from this disorder. But the jury would not accept this and he was found guilty of murder with malice.

That there may be a relationship between epilepsy and murder has been shown by a study at Maudsley Hospital in London. Out of more than a hundred murderers examined, over seventeen percent had epilepsy, compared with 0.5 per cent for the normal population.

EFFECTS
● In insane automatism the effects often vary with the patient. With non-insane automatism, sleepwalking, the subject looks awake, moves about and has open eyes. But sleepwalkers rarely respond if spoken to and seem to be engaged in a set pattern of behaviour. Experiments have shown that their brain waves in this condition show the pattern of sleep.

REAL-LIFE EXAMPLES
● One night in May, 1987, Ken Parks drove fourteen miles from his home in Toronto, Canada, to his in-laws' house where he stabbed his mother-in-law to death and gravely injured his father-in-law. The remarkable defence of sleepwalking (Parks had been a victim of it all his life), succeeded for the first time in Canada and Parks was found not guilty.
● An early defence of epileptic automatism was put forward by the redoubtable defender Sir Edward Marshall Hall, in February, 1926, for Lock Ah Tam, a Chinese man who lived in Liverpool and who admitted to killing his wife and children. But it was to take another 30 years before the 1957 Homicide Act introduced the defence of diminished responsibility (*see* MANSLAUGHTER page 130) and he was hanged.

2 AXE

Availability 5/10
Effectiveness 9/10
Detectability 8/10

Because of its heavy weight and sharp edge, the axe is a truly horrific weapon and its association with the executioner makes it a potent symbol in crime fiction. In earlier days, before gas fires and electric heating, an axe would be found in every household, for chopping wood, and thus was conveniently to hand as a murder weapon.

EFFECTS
● The wounds inflicted by the sharp edge of an axe can be fearsome. The flat end will give wounds not very different from any other BLUNT INSTRUMENT (*see* page 15). And both types of wounds are usually found on the head or upper torso of the victim. The sharp edge will usually leave a cleft, into which the weapon can be fitted afterwards to help identify it. Since the sharp edge always splits the skin and underlying tissues, and fragments bone, the wounds are also accompanied by liberal quantities of blood. This can be spashed everywhere, including on the murderer and his clothes, a fact often forgotten by fiction writers. And, since an attack with an axe is usually done in a rage and on the spur of the moment, it makes little sense to have the murderer undress first, as was suggested by the prosecution in the Wallace case in April, 1931.

REAL-LIFE EXAMPLES
● In 1889, in New York State, Roxanne Druse killed her farmer husband and used the axe to help with the DISPOSAL OF THE BODY (*see* page 20).
● The well-known Lizzie Borden, according to the rhyme, '...gave her mother forty whacks' (with an axe) in Fall River, Massachusetts in 1893.
● One would think that a serial killer using an axe to smash into people's homes at night and then murdering the occupants with it would easily be caught. But between 1911 and 1919 an axe-man terrorised the Italian community on New Orleans, killing nine people. And though the murderer nearly always left the axe behind, he was never caught.
● In July 1993, David Masters, a veterinary surgeon, killed his wife with twelve blows of an axe while she was asleep in their Wiltshire home. He then committed suicide.

2 BACTERIAL POISONING	Availability	2/10
	Effectiveness	5/10
	Detectability	2/10

The advantage to crime-writers and murderers alike is that death by deliberate bacterial poisoning can only with difficulty be distinguished from death from natural causes or accidental death, but it is difficult to arrange.

Bacteria are primitive forms of microscopic organisms, not all of which are harmful to humans. Those that are produce toxins which are harmful to tissues, such as the bacteria in diphtheria, typhoid and tuberculosis. Botulism poisoning arises from a toxin in the bacterium *Clostridium botulinum*, which can be present in food – though it is easily destroyed by cooking. The toxin kills some 50 per cent of its victims. Salmonella, another bacterial food poisoning agent, is lethal in only one per cent of cases,

Bacteria can be grown artificially (cultured) on a nutrient medium, such as gelatin or milk in the bottom of a Petri dish, a flat round glass dish covered with a glass plate. The medium is innoculated with bacterial material, then incubated for several days at body temperature, in an oven. This technique is also used to help identify the bacterium.

EFFECTS
- Botulism can occur in improperly canned meat, fish and vegetables and the toxin is tasteless and odourless. It causes double vision, muscle paralysis, nausea and vomiting, although the effects are usually delayed for eight to twenty-four hours and death can take as long as eight days to occur.

REAL-LIFE EXAMPLES
- Henri Girard, a crooked French financier, known as the First Scientific Murderer, killed several people between 1912 and 1918 by administering typhoid bacteria in water and by injection.
- In March, 1969, the wife of Dr John Hill, a plastic surgeon in Houston, Texas, died, it was afterwards said, from the administration by her husband of a bacterial culture, made from 'every form of human excretion'. But, before he could be properly tried, Dr Hill was killed by an assassin apparently bought by his wife's oil millionaire father.

FICTIONAL EXAMPLES
- In Alisa Craig's *A Pint of Murder* the victim died from eating food from a can which had not been properly heated.
- In a TV episode of *Murder She Wrote* a doctored jar of preserves in a restaurant was used as the murder weapon.

2 BLUNT INSTRUMENTS

Availability	9/10
Effectiveness	4/10
Detectability	9/10

This is one of the commonest methods of murder, and the instruments used have ranged from household implements such as pokers or articles of furniture and ornaments to tyre-irons, jacks, stones and rocks, a golf tee and even a policeman's truncheon. In other words, almost anything which is handy – and heavy enough. For this method is usually one of impulse. It can be premeditated, but far more often it is the result of sudden fury or sometimes fear, where for example a burglar batters a householder he has inadvertently woken up and who won't stop screaming. It is also one of the most inefficient. A single blow to the head will very rarely kill a person. It probably won't even render them unconscious. A rain of blows, again to the head, is usually necessary and even then it probably won't keep them quiet. Many bludgeoning murderers have resorted to throat cutting to finally finish off the victims.

EFFECTS
- Heavy blows to the head cause laceration of the tissues and, if heavy enough, fractures of the skull. These can be simple cracks in the bones or complicated depressed fractures, depending on the weapon used. A great deal of blood is lost which will splash on to the surrounding walls if in a room and even on to the ceiling and also on to the attacker. The weapon itself will also have blood, tissue, hair and sometimes fragments of bone adhering to it. Death will be from brain injury, which can occur without the skull being fractured, though in this case several hours or even days can pass before death intervenes.

REAL-LIFE CASES
- Millionaire Sir Harry Oakes was found battered to death and set on fire at his home in the Bahamas in 1943. The weapon, which left four triangular-shaped marks on his head was never found and neither was the murderer.
- Another unsolved blunt instrument crime was the killing of the wife of Dr Sheppard in Cleveland, Ohio in 1954. He was originally found guilty of her murder but, ten years later, acquitted after a retrial.
- Two New Zealand teenagers, Pauline Parker and Juliet Hulme, killed Mrs Parker with a brick held in a stocking in 1954. It took some forty blows to do it. They were found guilty and sentenced to be detained at Her Majesty's pleasure.

FICTIONAL EXAMPLES
- Catherine Aird uses a variation of the theme of the heavy object falling on the victim's head by having a piece of statuary dislodged by a Foucault's pendulum in *His Burial Too*.

15

2 BURNING

Availability	8/10
Effectiveness	8/10
Detectability	7/10

Murder by burning used to be rare, but it has become distressingly more common with several recent cases of burglars tying up householders and setting fire to them as they depart so as to leave behind no witnesses. Modern medicine suggests that burning which destroys more than 70 per cent of the skin of a young healthy person is likely to prove fatal, but with an elderly person this can be reduced to 30 per cent. Over the years it has become more common to find bodies which have been set on fire after death either to disguise another cause of death, such as poison, or to conceal the identity of the victim. In the early days of motor cars, two car owners set fire to their vehicles with bodies in them to try and make it appear that they themselves had perished in the flames. Yet another reason for burning a body is to get rid of it (DISPOSAL OF THE BODY *see* page 20).

EFFECTS
- Burning bodies take up what is known as a 'pugilistic attitude', due to the stiffening and contraction of the muscles with the heat. There are also a number of tests which can be done to determine whether the body was alive when burning began.
- The presence of carbon monoxide in the blood indicates that the person was breathing when the fire started and this can be confirmed by the presence of fine particles of soot in the lungs. Whether burn injuries were suffered before or after death can also be shown by the presence or absence of 'vital signs'. Burns to a living body will be accompanied by inflammation near the injury and the presence of blistering, fluid from which will contain proteins. Burns inflicted after death are hard and yellowish and blisters, if formed, will contain little fluid, which will not yield proteins.

REAL-LIFE EXAMPLES
- Alfred Rouse confessed in 1931, after he had been convicted and just before he was hanged, that he had picked up a tramp in his car, knocked him unconscious and set fire to the car with the man inside. The identity of the tramp was never established. A similar case occurred in 1929 in Regensburg in Germany.
- George Stephenson and the two Daly brothers burst into a mansion near Fordingbridge in Hampshire, one evening in 1987 and tied up five people, a retired publisher and his invalid wife, their son and his wife and an elderly housekeeper. They ransacked the house, put the victims into a bedroom and doused them and the furniture with petrol. As they left, they tossed a firelighter into a room. All five victims died.

2 CROSSBOWS

Availability	9/10
Effectiveness	8/10
Detectability	9/10

The difference between the crossbow and the longbow (of Robin Hood fame, or the archers of the Battle of Crécy, or the bows and arrows of our youth) is that in the crossbow the bow is horizontal. Another is that in the crossbow the string is pulled back mechanically and thus does not require the strength of an arm needed to fire the longbow. They were used in battle in medieval times until they were outranged by the longbow, which also took less time to fire, and so they gradually fell out of use.

Today, crossbows are considerably more powerful and sophisticated. Some have telescopic sights, but their accuracy range is normally around 15 to 20 yards. They have 40 to 50 pounds of draw weight tension on the bow and the six-inch bolts are made of steel. Yet they are readily available in many sports shops.

EFFECTS
● While they do not have the penetrating power and propensity for tissue damage of pistol bullets, crossbow bolts, fired from close range, can kill if they hit a vital part of the body. And crossbows are far quieter than hand-guns.

REAL-LIFE EXAMPLES
● When Marie Witte was caught by her mother-in-law cashing cheques on the old lady's bank account in Trail Creek, Indiana, in 1983, she decided to kill her. She nominated her youngest son to do the job as he was a juvenile and would be treated more leniently should the crime be brought home to him. He shot the old lady with his sports crossbow while she was asleep. When questioned by the police he readily admitted everything and his mother was sentenced to 90 years in jail.
● In July, 1988, thirty-five-year-old Diana Maw was found slumped outside her top-floor flat in Ealing, West London. She had been shot with a crossbow bolt which had hit her neck behind the right ear and severed the spinal column. The killer was never discovered.

FICTIONAL EXAMPLES
● A crossbow is used to kill a number of people in David Hilton's *The Hyte Manoeuvre*. The same method is employed in one of John Dickson Carr's most famous locked-room murders, *The Judas Window*.

2 DEFENESTRATION

Availability	3/10
Effectiveness	9/10
Detectability	2/10

This means literally pushing someone out of a window, but can be taken in this context as any fatal fall from a high place, such as a building, a cliff, etc. Suicides and, less commonly, accidents account for a proportion of deaths from such falls but the efficiency of this method from the point of view of crime-writers is that it is extremely difficult to tell: did he jump, or was he pushed? Obviously, suicides may leave a note or letter or there may be a witness. Often, would-be suicides who leap from high buildings (called 'jumpers' in America), wait for quite some time and a crowd will collect below to watch.

EFFECTS
● Speeds of up to 70 mph can be reached by a body falling from a height and this can result in massive impact injuries. Hitting the ground head first will produce skull, neck and spinal injuries and feet-first landings will result in the breaking and telescoping of the legs. The surface does not even have to be hard. After one or two hundred feet even water will cause fatal injuries.
● Reconstructions of the incident may help in detecting homicide, using, for example, an anthropometric dummy of the same size and weight as the victim. This will help to determine the trajectory of the fall since a body always falls in an arc. A powerful man who threw his wife off a balcony in Baltimore was convicted because she landed some sixteen feet away from the building a distance she couldn't possibly have jumped.

REAL-LIFE EXAMPLES
● The famous case of Helen Smith is still unsolved. She was a young nurse working at a hospital in Jeddah, Saudi Arabia. After a party on the sixth-floor of an apartment building, in May 1979, she was found dead, having apparently fallen from the balcony. Nearby was the body of a Dutch seaman impaled on the railings. The story given out was that the pair had gone on to the balcony to make love and must have fallen off. But Ron Smith, Helen's father, still maintains that she was murdered.
● In October, 1949, Donald Hume killed Stanley Setty, dismembered his body and dropped a parcel containing the torso from an aeroplane over the North Sea. But it was washed ashore and the pathologist recognised the injuries the torso had sustained as being similar to those he had seen in the war when people had fallen out of planes and landed without a parachute. Hume was convicted of manslaughter.

2 DISPOSAL OF THE BODY I

Availability	8/10
Effectiveness	4/10
Detectability	8/10

This is an extremely important part of the process. But it is where real-life situations and fictional ones can differ considerably. For a premeditating murderer, getting rid of the body offers considerable advantages. If it can be successfully concealed or destroyed it makes the subsequent investigation very difficult. Even if the concealment only delays the start of an inquiry it will give time for the perpetrator to destroy vital evidence or set up an alibi. But in crime fiction if there is no body there is usually no story. Occasionally, there appear stories about the search for a missing person but a fictional murder investigation nearly always has a corpse.

Nevertheless, the ways in which real murderers have attempted to get rid of bodies often give useful ideas for fiction writers. I therefore list a number of the more important methods.

ACIDS
- A number of strong liquid acids have been used by murderers to destroy bodies. Hydrochloric Acid (Spirits of Salts) is a powerful reagent which was used by chauffeur Erwin Spengler in 1987 to dispose of the cut-up portions of the body of his employer Frau Kornagel. He then flushed the solution down the bath in her home on Lake Constance.
- Sulphuric Acid (Oil of Vitriol) was favoured by Haigh, up to his capture in 1949, to get rid of a number of bodies in oil drums in a rented garage. But the acid did not dissolve the gall stones of his final victim and this helped to identify her.

CAUSTIC POTASH
- On heating, this dissolves body fat much more easily than many acids, but is slower on the rest of the body. However, it was employed by Chicago businessman Adolph Luetgart in 1897 to dispose of the body of his wife in a steam-heated vat used for making sausage meat.

QUICKLIME
- The powder Quicklime (calcium oxide) is normally made by heating slaked lime (calcium hydroxide). It will attack flesh, but its efficiency is much reduced if it is allowed to take up water from the air or the surrounding soil to return to slaked lime, which actually has a mild preserving effect. Though it has been used reasonably successfully (Dr Crippen, 1910, and Dr Petiot, 1944), some murderers have come unstuck, notably Henry Dobkin, 1942, whose use of the material helped to preserve the voice-box of his wife's body, from which it was proved that she died from STRANGULATION (*see* page 65).

2 DISPOSAL OF THE BODY II

Availability	8/10
Effectiveness	4/10
Detectability	8/10

DISMEMBERMENT

● This may be done either to make the corpse unrecognisable, to facilitate its transport or as a preliminary step to other methods of disposal. Dr Buck Ruxton cut up the bodies of his wife and the maid into 70 pieces and distributed them along a stream, just north of Moffat in Scotland. But remarkable forensic work managed to prove the identity of both. Dismemberment may take several hours and require some skill in butchery and a callousness most people do not have, but it can be effective, as in the case of Dennis Nilsen, who successfully disposed of thirteen bodies before making the mistakes which led to his capture.

BURNING

● Surprisingly, this is an efficient way of getting rid of a body, but it can take a long time. Nilsen burnt the remains of several bodies on a large bonfire he made on some waste ground.

● Henri Landru is thought to have disposed of ten women and one youth in a large kitchen stove and no trace of them was ever found.

●'Big Harry' McKenny and John Childs dismembered and burnt several bodies on the living room fire of a council flat in Poplar.

BURYING OR INTERRING

● Probably the most popular method of body disposal and one of the most successful. Even back-garden burials can remain hidden for a long time, as the recent case of Fred and Rosemary West shows.

● Ian Brady and Myra Hindley buried several bodies on Saddleworth Moor and were subsequently unable to locate the grave of one of their victims. On the other hand, a shallow grave in a relatively well-populated area stands a good chance of being discovered.

LAKES

● Deep lakes have always exerted a fascination on murderers. But these days there is always the chance of amateur scuba-divers discovering the body, as happened a few years ago with bodies dumped in Wastwater and Crummock Water in the Lake District.

WHAT HAPPENS IF NO BODY IS FOUND?

● The Hosein brothers kidnapped Mrs Muriel McKay. Her body was never found although it has been supposed that they fed it to their pigs.

● Michael Onufrejczyk, an ex-Polish soldier, killed his business partner on a farm in Wales, but the body was never discovered.

● James Camb, a ship's steward, confessed that he had pushed the body of actress Gay Gibson out of a porthole, and her body was not recovered. In all three cases the accused were still convicted of murder.

2 DROWNING

Availability	9/10
Effectiveness	6/10
Detectability	5/10

In spite of the ready availability of water – people can drown in a bath or even in a puddle – murder by drowning is not common. The majority of deaths are accidental: boating accidents, children tumbling into rivers or ponds or drunks falling into water. Death by drowning can be caused in two ways: 'dry drowning' in which water in the throat or the sudden immersion of a body in cold water induces a constriction and closing of the airways (laryngeal spasm) or a cardiac arrest: or the much more common 'wet drowning' in which ASPHYXIATION (*see* page 11) is induced by the presence of large volumes of water in the lungs. This can take five minutes or more, with the victims frantically holding their breaths until they have to let go and the in-rush of water causes further panic and struggling. The lungs eventually become waterlogged and the body sinks to the bottom. Death is more rapid in fresh than salt water because fresh water more readily enters the blood stream, upsetting the sodium/potassium balance, which leads to rapid and irregular beating of the heart (ventricular fibrillation) which, in turn, hastens death. Salt water has a higher osmotic pressure and does not diffuse into the blood stream so easily.

EFFECTS
- There are few external signs of drowning. A fine white foam sometimes appears at the nostrils and mouth and for bodies which have been immersed for some time, wrinkling of the hands ('washerwoman's hands') and feet will occur. Objects may be clasped in the dead person's hands, such as water weeds or stones which the drowned victim gripped in their death throes. The body may sustain injuries due to being bumped about on rocks, but these will usually occur after death. It is relatively easy for a pathologist to determine if a body was alive when immersed, because both sea and fresh water contain microscopic algae called diatoms which, during the drowning process, pass into the bloodstream, heart, lungs and even the bone marrow, whereas a dead body dumped in water will only have a few, usually in the throat.

REAL-LIFE EXAMPLES
- Denis Nilsen, during his London killing spree of 1978-1983, despatched two of his fifteen victims by making them insensible through drink and then putting their heads in a bucket of water.
- George Smith, the Brides in the Bath murderer, killed his young wives by a process demonstrated by pathologist Bernard Spilsbury and Inspector Neil at Smith's trial in 1915. By pulling on the women's legs while they were in a hip bath he forced their heads under the water and unconsciousness and death soon followed.

FICTIONAL EXAMPLES
- In Ross Macdonald's *The Doomsters* a woman is stunned with a wine bottle and then dumped in the sea to simulate suicide.

2 ELECTROCUTION

Availability	9/10
Effectiveness	5/10
Detectability	6/10

Electrocution is one of the most common methods of domestic murder. An electric heater thrown into the bath; the tub wired up to the mains; a metal soap dish connected to the mains; a tampered-with electric lawn mower; all these have been tried. Not always with success, it must be said, for this is not the most reliable method of murder.

EFFECTS

● These depend a great deal on the type of current. Direct Current (DC), from batteries, causes more tissue damage and burns, but is not as dangerous as Alternating Current (AC). The ordinary British domestic supply is 220 volts AC, which causes the heart muscles to quiver (ventricular fibrillation), reducing its pumping action, and death follows quickly. Electricity must also pass into and out of the body and it makes a difference what path it takes. In one leg and out of the other is less dangerous than hand to leg or head to leg, because the current then passes through vital organs like the heart.

● The contact with the source of electricity is also important. Electricity passes more easily through water than dry air and a poor or momentary contact will enable people to survive over 1000 volts, which would normally kill. This is also why most electrical deaths occur in the bathroom or kitchen.

● After death, burn marks are usually seen at the entrance and exit points. The burns can be severe, including charring of the skin, or simply a characteristic pale area with a lilac ring surrounding the spot. Sometimes there are no marks at all.

REAL-LIFE EXAMPLES

● In 1993, Peter Ellis, a Cardiff property developer, heavily insured his wife then connected her bath to the household mains. But the discharge threw her out of the bath and she survived.

● In Germany, Karl Kasper, in 1972, electrocuted his wife by wiring her up to the mains, then claimed it was done accidentally during a sex game. But he had also just insured his wife and he was sentenced to twelve years.

FICTIONAL EXAMPLES

● In a TV episode of *Inspector Morse* 'Deceived By Flight', written by Anthony Minghella from an idea by Colin Dexter, a lawyer is electrocuted by having a live radio lead placed in his mouth while he is under sedatives.

2 EMBOLISM (AIR)

Availability	3/10
Effectiveness	8/10
Detectability	2/10

Embolism is the condition where a blood vessel becomes blocked, by a clot of blood, a globule of fat or other substance, or a bubble of air. If the flow of blood to the heart or brain is stopped then death quickly results. As a method of murder the air usually needs to be injected with a syringe into the blood stream and therefore requires the kind of skill possessed by a doctor, a nurse or even someone used to injecting themselves such as a drug addict. It is a popular opinion that a minute air bubble injected into a vein will cause death, but this is not so. For anyone sick or elderly around 40cc of air, about an egg-cupful, might be enough, but for a fit healthy person around 300cc, about half a pint, would be required. So a mighty large syringe would be needed.

EFFECTS
- An air embolism in the brain would result in coma and, if it occurred elsewhere, the death might look like heart failure. But there would be very little evidence of the real cause of death, although some pathologists believe that a froth observed in the heart during autopsy and in blood vessels would be an indication of an air embolism.

REAL-LIFE EXAMPLES
- Dr Herman Sander injected 40cc of air into a cancer patient in New Hampshire, USA, in 1949. He then made out a death certificate giving cancer of the bowel as the cause of death. But in the case notes he detailed what he had actually done and was put on trial for murder. The trial created a sensation and was called a mercy killing, but Dr Sander claimed his patient was already dead when he injected the air, 'just to make sure'. He was found not guilty.
- Accidental air embolisms can also occur from wounds in the neck or during surgery in that region and some cases of back-street abortionists causing death by air embolism have been detailed. Careless use of the Higginson syringe, which is used to inject soapy water into the womb, can cause air to be forced into the womb which can sometimes enter the pregnant woman's blood stream resulting in death.

FICTIONAL EXAMPLES
- In Dorothy Sayers' *Unnatural Death,* Lord Peter Wimsey discovered that a woman had caused the deaths of a number of people by injecting air into them. All the deaths were initially ascribed to heart failure.

2 EXPLOSIVES

Availability	5/10
Effectiveness	7/10
Detectability	9/10

Many substances can be used to make bombs, including petrol, some household cleaners and agricultural fertilisers; and the principles of making a crude bomb can be learned from applied chemistry textbooks. Explosives are of two types: low explosives such as gunpowder and powders used in gun cartridges (FIREARMS *see* page 25) and high explosives such as TNT, dynamite and Semtex. High explosives require a small explosion to set them off, for example from a blasting cap activated by a fuse or a battery. Some expertise is necessary in handling explosives, for sticks of dynamite can be very unstable. Lethal bombs have been made in cigarette packets, letters and hollowed-out books, which can be filled with explosives and sent through the post.

EFFECTS

● With even a small amount of high explosive (two or four pounds) the effects on anyone standing close to the site of the detonation and unprotected by walls are catastrophic. The body will literally be torn apart. Further away, lethal injuries may be sustained by blast, fragments from the bomb-casing (shrapnel), flying glass or building debris. The sheer destructive power of explosives have made them favoured weapons for terrorists, although some murderers have used explosives on a more personal level.

REAL-LIFE EXAMPLES

● Graham Backhouse, a Cotswold farmer, set up an ingenious scheme in 1984 to kill his wife and collect on the life insurance. He used a car bomb apparently intended for himself, but owing to the sturdy construction of the Volvo estate, his wife survived the attack.

● Steve Benson killed his mother and younger brother with a bomb placed in their car in Florida in 1985, but his sister had just opened the car door before the explosion and she survived the blast.

● Albert Guay caused a bomb to be placed aboard a plane his wife was taking on a internal flight in Canada in 1949. The explosion led to the plane crashing killing his wife and 22 other people.

FICTIONAL EXAMPLES

● In William Le Queux's *England's Peril*, Lord Casterton is the victim of an exploding cigar.

2 FIREARMS (SMOOTH BORE)

Availability	3/10
Effectiveness	8/10
Detectability	7/10

Firearms can be divided into SMOOTH BORE in which the inside of the barrel is smooth, and RIFLED in which it is not (see page 26). In SMOOTH BORE arms, the diameter of the inside of the barrel, called the calibre or bore, is taken as the number of spherical lead balls, one of which will just fit inside the barrel, and which make up one pound weight. If it needs 12 of these to weigh one pound the weapon is called a 12 bore or 12 gauge. Smooth bore weapons are usually shotguns or sporting guns and are used to shoot wildfowl, rabbits, etc. They can be single or double-barrelled, and in the latter case the barrels are either side by side or one on top of the other (called over and under).

The guns can also be single-shot weapons which 'break' just beyond the stock or butt so that the barrel drops down and the fired cartridges can be extracted and the gun reloaded by hand. Slide or pump-action shotguns have a slide beneath the barrel which, when moved backwards and forwards, automatically positions another cartridge in the firing chamber and closes the breech. This type usually ejects the cartridge after firing. With the so-called 'sawn-off' shot guns, the barrel or barrels are cut down to about a foot in length and the stock is also reduced to make the weapon more easily concealed. This type is favoured by bank robbers. Shotguns normally have a range of about 50 yards. Ownership requires a licence.

Shotgun cartridges consist of a cardboard or plastic cylinder about 2½ inches long loaded with small lead pellets or shot. The base is brass with a detonating charge at its centre and the shot is held above the propellant charge by cardboard felt or plastic discs called wads.

EFFECTS
● At close range the shotgun is a devastating weapon, inflicting massive bodily damage. But the lethal range of a shotgun is probably under fifteen yards, depending on what part of the body is hit. For information on the spreading of shot when the gun is fired, see GUNSHOT WOUNDS (page 90).

REAL-LIFE EXAMPLES
●In October, 1927, a poacher fired on two gamekeepers near Bath, killing one. The other gamekeeper fired at the fleeing poacher. The poacher later claimed that he only fired after being shot himself. But the pattern of indentations on his back showed he had been 15 yards away when he was hit, whereas the charge which killed the gamekeeper was proved, by the lack of scatter of the shot, to have been fired from less than five yards.

THE CRIME WRITER'S HANDBOOK

2 FIREARMS (RIFLED) HANDGUNS

Availability	2/10
Effectiveness	7/10
Detectability	8/10

For an explanation of rifling see BALLISTICS (page 70). The calibre of rifled weapons (*see* page 25), in Britain and the United States, is measured in decimals of one inch, e.g. .22, .303, .455, etc. On the Continent, the measurements are in millimetres. Rifled weapons may be short-barrelled handguns (1 to 12 inches), long-barrelled rifles (2 to 3 feet), machine and sub-machine guns. After the Dunblane massacre of 1996, 80% of all handguns were banned from non-professional use. At the time of publication, .22 weapons are not banned, but eventually will be.

Handguns are either revolvers or pistols. Revolvers have a cylindrical magazine containing five or six chambers, each housing one cartridge. Pulling the hammer back with the thumb (cocking it) brings the next chamber into the firing position. This is the single action revolver. Double action weapons are cocked by exerting pressure on the trigger, though they can be cocked by hand. Revolvers are robust weapons and most police forces in America are armed with the Smith & Wesson .38 revolver.

Pistols have a sealed-in chamber which is part of the barrel and a hollow butt into which the magazine can be fitted. They are popularly known as 'automatics', although more accurately called 'self-loading' or 'semi-automatics'. The spent cartridge is ejected mechanically, unlike the revolver where the cartridge must be ejected manually. Single-shot pistols require manual loading each time the gun is fired. The Derringer is a popular example and can have one or more barrels, each of which is loaded and fired separately.

The modern cartridge consists of a metal cylinder designed to fit a particular gun-chamber and is rimmed for extraction in a revolver or is rimless for automatics. In the centre of the base, a soft metal cap contains a primer charge which is crushed by the gun's firing pin setting off the main propellant, a smokeless type based on nitrocellulose and nitroglycerine. Both primer and propellant leave detectable traces on close-range targets and the hand of the firer. Lead bullets are usually jacketed with cupro-nickel and cemented into the top of the cartridge case.

EFFECTS
● The typical appearance of an entry wound is a small, circular or oval hole surrounded by an inflamed ring of abraded skin. Blood loss is usually slight. An exit wound will be larger than the entry wound. See also GUNSHOT WOUNDS (page 90).

REAL-LIFE EXAMPLES
● David Berkowitz, New York's 'Son of Sam' killer, shot six people between 1976 and 77, with a .44 Bulldog revolver.

2 FIREARMS (RIFLED) RIFLES AND MACHINE PISTOLS

Availability   2/10
Effectiveness   8/10
Detectability   8/10

Rifles are fired from the shoulder and the long barrel and the rifling in the barrel makes them accurate up to ranges of 3,000 yards. Fitted with telescopic or infra-red sights, the rifle is the favoured weapon of the assassin or 'hit man' who wishes to kill at long range. Both John F. Kennedy and Martin Luther King were killed by rifle bullets. Rifles come in a number of categories: sporting, military, target and small-bore target rifles. These are then further subdivided according to the method of re-loading. Single shot require loading after each discharge, like single shot pistols. Mechanical forms of loading and ejection of cartridges inlude: lever action, bolt action and pump or slide action, which is similar to that used for shotguns. Rifles can also be classified as 'automatics', but, as with pistols, are not true automatics unless the weapon keeps on firing so long as the trigger is pressed. Where the trigger must be pressed each time a bullet is fired they are referred to as self-loading or semi-automatic. Cartridges: *see* HANDGUNS (page 26).

Machine and sub-machine guns are sometimes known as 'machine pistols' and can be true automatics or semi-automatics. They fire pistol ammunition, but usually require two hands to hold them. The heavier military versions need supporting on a tripod. The old-style American gangsters used Thompson sub-machine guns, but they are not common today.

EFFECTS
● The effects of a rifle bullet are similar to that of a handgun bullet except where the higher muzzle velocity of the rifle creates a larger wound. The Armalite rifle fires a small calibre bullet which 'tumbles' when it hits, causing extensive tissue damage. See also GUNSHOT WOUNDS (page 90).

REAL-LIFE EXAMPLES
● Jeremy Bamber used a .22 semi-automatic Anschutz rifle fitted with a silencer to kill his adopted father, mother, sister and two young nephews at White House Farm in Essex in August, 1985. He then claimed that a phone call he'd received indicated that his sister had killed them all and then committed suicide. But the rifle barrel, including the silencer, was too long for her to have been able to reach the trigger and still shoot herself in the head, and he was convicted of murder.
● In 1984, a Denver radio talk-show host was shot by a .45MAC10 machine pistol.

2 HANGING

Availability	7/10
Effectiveness	8/10
Detectability	8/10

This is very similar to STRANGULATION (*see* page 65) by means of a ligature, with the force being supplied by the weight of the body itself. But death can result from two different causes. In the humaner kinds of judicial hanging the noose is positioned under the left ear and the subject falls, in a carefully calculated drop, through a trap door. This forces the noose round to the front, jerking the head back and fracturing or dislocating the vertebrae near the brain, causing almost instantaneous death. But death can also occur with an incorrectly placed noose and even with no drop at all. Many suicides hang themselves without their feet leaving the ground or floor, simply by securing the rope with the noose round their necks and leaning on it. Compression of the neck causes unconsciousness and the victim dies from slow strangulation.

EFFECTS
● Strangulation with a ligature usually produces a mark round the neck which is horizontal. With hanging, the mark slopes upward towards the position of the suspending rope. Apart from this the signs are very similar to those from strangulation and ASPHYXIA (*see* page 11).

Accidental hangings have occurred as a result of the masochistic sexual practice known as auto-erotic asphyxia, in which some people, usually men, deliberately restrict oxygen to the brain to enhance orgasm. This can usually be seen by the presence of pornographic literature near by, for example, or the fact that the victim is naked, dressed in women's clothes or fetishistic bondage equipment. The ligature is often padded to prevent bruising of the neck.

REAL-LIFE EXAMPLES
● In November, 1953, Sergeant Emmett-Dunne of the occupying forces in Germany killed fellow sergeant Reginald Watters with a Karate type blow to the Adam's Apple (*see* also KARATE page 31). He then strung the body up over the stairwell in the barracks to make it look like suicide, which was the subsequent inquest verdict. But Emmett-Dunne then made the mistake of marrying Watters' widow. Suspicions were aroused, the body exhumed and another autopsy conducted, this time by eminent pathologist Dr F.E. Camps, who discovered the real cause of death. Emmett-Dunne received life imprisonment.
● In 1994, Conservative MP Steven Milligan died as a result of auto-erotic asphyxia.

2 HIT-AND-RUN

Availability	8/10
Effectiveness	5/10
Detectability	7/10

The invention of the motor-car presented murderers (and crime writers) with an entirely new weapon. Everybody knows that you can be killed by being knocked down by a car. What better method could be devised than to run the victim down and, if the car was afterwards traced, claim it was an accident? The trouble is that being hit by a car, even at a considerable speed, is no guarantee that the person will be killed. They'd suffer considerable injuries, undoubtedly, but they might survive to describe the car and who was driving it. Better perhaps to render the victim unconscious and then lay them in the road and run the car over them. This has been tried a few times, once by a Glasgow policeman – a PC Robertson in 1950 – without conspicuous success, because the injuries sustained are not the same as being hit by a car at speed.

A rather more effective method of murder, though perhaps not strictly 'hit-and-run' is to render the victim unconscious, place them in a car and run the car over a cliff though finding a suitable location may be a problem.

EFFECTS
- An upright person will nearly always sustain considerable injuries to both legs on being hit by a car, and usually head and internal injuries will occur as the body is thrown up on to the vehicle's bonnet and possibly hits the windscreen. The car will nearly always leave traces both on the body and at the scene. Tyre marks, paint flakes, pieces of broken glass from the headlamps and pieces of trim and other ornamentation all give the forensic scientist ample evidence to work with.

REAL-LIFE EXAMPLES
- Charles Mortimer, a lance corporal in the Welsh regiment, stole a car one August day in 1935 and drove around the country lanes deliberately knocking people off their cycles. One girl landed on the bonnet, was carried along until she slid off over the parapet of a bridge and afterwards died. Mortimer was convicted of murder, but reprieved because of his obvious mental instability.
- South African, Carolyn Laurens, ensured that her husband was drunk, then drove their car into a ravine, jumping clear just in time. She would have got away with it too, except that she subsequently killed her sister and then confessed to both crimes.

FICTIONAL EXAMPLE
- In Sheila Radley's *Who Saw Him Die* (1987) a well-known drunk is run over and killed as he staggers across the street at closing time. Is it an accident or murder?

2 IMPOSSIBILITIES AND MISCELLANEOUS METHODS OF MURDER

There are a number of ingenious murder weapons used by fiction writers in the past, which frankly strain credulity. The ice bullet is one. It would not be difficult to cast a bullet of ice, but firing it from a gun would simply melt the ice before it reached its target, if not before it even left the gun barrel. An ice dagger is more practical – a stalactite might be used to stab someone and then the heat of the body would reduce the ice to water and thus the weapon would disappear.

Causing someone to eat powdered glass has also been suggested as a murder technique. In fact, the well-known forensic chemist, Roche Lynch, stated that he had come across attempts to use it. But the writer who quotes him, Brian Lane in *The Encyclopedia of Forensic Science,* also says that he personally has never come across a case of powdered glass being fatal. Edith Thompson wrote to her lover, Frederick Bywaters, to say that she had used it on her husband. But the post-mortem on him after Bywaters had stabbed him to death in 1922, showed no sign of his ever having eaten powdered glass. Like other things which appeared in her letters it was undoubtedly a figment of her over-active imagination.

REAL-LIFE EXAMPLES
- Injuries may be caused by fragments of glass. In 1988 Rodney Whitchelo, a former police detective, spiked cans of pet food and jars of baby food and pickles, with, among other things, cut-up razor blades and sharp pieces of glass, then tried to blackmail the companies concerned, Pedigree Petfoods, Heinz and Cow and Gate. He even succeeded in cutting a baby's mouth with a sliver of razor blade he had concealed in a jar of pear-flavoured yoghurt and the child needed hospital treatment. The companies paid out considerable sums in blackmail before he was finally caught.

FICTIONAL EXAMPLES
- Using a similar theme to the Whitchelo case, Andrew Puckett, in *Bloodhound*, has a blackmailer contaminate blood transfusion packs with the bacterium *Serratia liquefaciens*, which when transfused causes death by post-transfusion septicaemia. He then demanded one million pounds from the National Blood Transfusion Service. *See* also BACTERIAL POISONING (page 14).

- Roald Dahl gives one of his heroines a frozen leg of lamb with which to club her husband to death – and then has her cook it for the detectives conducting the investigation. She has to hide her giggles when one of them, having just complimented her on her cooking, comments that he's convinced the murder weapon must be right under their noses.

2 KARATE

Availability 3/10
Effectiveness 9/10
Detectability 3/10

You can kill quite easily with a karate 'chop' to the front of the neck delivered with the outside edge of the hand. This was one of the 'silent kill' methods taught to commandos during the Second World War and also to troops undergoing training in unarmed combat. It requires some skill and thus is not available to everybody, but anyone who has had some training should be capable of doing it. The blow itself is extremely powerful, being the result of a swinging action generating a lot of energy and delivered through a small area – the edge of the hand. Such blows can break bricks. Karate chops can be delivered to other parts of the body and it should also be remembered that karate is one of the martial arts and can also involve blows with the closed fists and kicking, all of which could be lethal in the hands of an expert. Apart from karate strikes, any heavy blows to the head or face delivered with the fist can also be fatal (*see* EFFECTS).

EFFECTS
● A karate chop to the front of the neck can compress the vagal nerve and cause the heart to stop quickly, *see* ASPHYXIA (page 11). Punching the face and head can cause fracture of the skull, brain damage and death. Fractured facial bones may also be driven into and break the skull with the same effects. Dislodgement of the teeth by blows and tearing of the soft tissues in the mouth and face can result in copious bleeding, which, especially if the victim is unconscious and lying down, may block the windpipe and cause asphyxiation.

REAL-LIFE EXAMPLES
● In May 1977, German karate expert Axel Roeder challenged his wife (who was also a karate expert) to a duel. He was jealous and angry, apparently, because she had danced with another man. It was subsequently found that she had ribs broken on both sides, her lungs were damaged, her liver was split and her stomach ruptured in four places. She died from internal bleeding.

FICTIONAL EXAMPLES
● Ngaio Marsh uses the karate chop very cleverly in *Off With His Head*.

2 KIDNAPPING

Availability	4/10
Effectiveness	5/10
Detectability	7/10

Literally 'unlawful seizure and detention', kidnapping is not strictly a method of murder, but is often unfortunately associated with the ultimate crime, since many kidnappers find it easier and more convenient to get rid of the victim. Kidnapping has had a long history, one of the first appearances of the word being in John Bunyan's *The Pilgrim's Progress* (1684). Motives for kidnapping may briefly be summarised as:

Slavery
● In the last century children were kidnapped and sent to serve as slaves on British plantations in America. Men were frequently kidnapped to serve in the British Navy (press-ganging). Women have often been seized for prostitution or to join harems.

Ransom
● Very common during the early years of the century in America, until the Lindbergh Act made it a federal offence. Still one of the most common motives.

Torture
● Occasionally, a victim may be abducted for the purposes of obtaining information, for revenge or to torture for pleasure, the latter being common among serial killers.

Political
● Many abductions during the 1970s were by terrorist groups.

Kidnapping requires planning and organisation and is rarely done by people acting alone, although Michael Sams (1992) and Donald Neilson (1976) probably acted on their own. These days, the British police take as their first priority the return unharmed of the victim and this usually means allowing the ransom to be paid. In the past the obvious presence of the police has scared off the kidnapper, possibly leading to the death of the victim. Many ingenious methods have been devised by kidnappers to ensure that the paying of the ransom does not lead to their detection. One of the most successful was that employed by Michael Sams.

REAL-LIFE EXAMPLES
● Hauptmann (1932 – convicted, probably unjustly, of the Lindbergh kidnapping).
● Hosein brothers (kidnapped and murdered Mrs Muriel McKay, 1970).
● In the 1980s, Philadelphian Gary Heidnik kidnapped black women for forced motherhood.

FICTIONAL EXAMPLES
● In Ross Macdonald's *The Moving Target* (1949) Californian oil magnate Sampson is kidnapped.

2 MASOCHISM	Availability	6/10
	Effectiveness	8/10
	Detectability	4/10

The word was invented by Professor von Krafft-Ebing who published one of the first accounts of sexual aberration, in 1898. It refers to sexual gratification obtained or increased by pain, humiliation or both, and can be inflicted either by the victim himself or herself or by another person. Krafft-Ebbing gave it as his opinion that it must eventually lead to the victim desiring to be killed by the person inflicting the pain. Whether this is true or not, it is certainly the case that a number of deaths have occurred during such activities, which might have been accidental or deliberate.

It is in fact a well-known sphere of operations among both male and female prostitutes and provides an easy option for many who offer sexual services as it does not involve the risks associated with direct sexual intercourse. But it can be extremely risky to the clients. The British police estimate there are at any one time some 40 to 50 unsolved gay murders on their files.

REAL-LIFE EXAMPLES
- Colin Ireland used to hang round gay bars in London in 1993, although he claimed that he was not homosexual. During a period of three months he picked up five gay men and went back to their homes with them. There, after persuading them to let him tie them up, he either strangled them or tied plastic bags over their heads. Then he stole money and credit cards from the apartments, Two he tortured to make them reveal their PIN numbers. But he was seen with his last victim by a British Transport Police video camera at Charing Cross station and, when the pictures were released to the press he went to the police.
- In February, 1987, a body fished out of the Waikato River in New Zealand was traced back to Neville Walker and teenaged Renee Chigwell who advertised herself as a 'Dominatrix'. She claimed that the victim had asked to be tied up, but died after being left with a dog-collar around his neck. The pathologist gave vagal inhibition (*see* ASPHYXIA page 11) as the cause of death, but Walker and Chigwell were both convicted of murder.

FICTIONAL EXAMPLES
- Christopher Isherwood's *Mr Norris Changes Trains* is about a masochist living in Berlin just after the First World War.

2 POISONS (INTRODUCTION)

Most people think of poisons as substances which when taken in small amounts result in death, and this is not a bad definition. But some substances, like morphine, are beneficial in very small amounts, but have very serious effects when larger doses are taken. Then there are many compounds, mainly plant extracts, which will make you ill, but are not lethal unless you are a young child or a sick elderly person. I have restricted the entries in this book to those substances which are considered to be the most poisonous, that is those which will kill in very small doses.

Many do not conform, however, to the usual picture of a poison, which is that the victim drinks a draft and, after a few dramatic facial contortions, dies immediately. Ricin, for example, is one of the most poisonous substances known. A gram (it is said) will kill 36,000 people, the population of a small town. Yet, in the only case of its use for homicide that I know of, the victim took four days to die and was able to describe how the poison had been administered and even made a good guess as to who had done it. It is important, for an accurate description of a poisoning, to know how long the chemical takes to work. The lethal dose will also vary. Roughly speaking, it depends on the body weight, so to kill a child requires much less than an adult. In each case described, I have calculated the fatal dose for an eleven-stone adult.

Doses are given for the pure dry substance:
1 milligram (mg) = 0.001 gram (g) or one thousandth of a gram.
1 kilogram (kg) = 1000 gram (g) or a thousand grams.
1 gram (g) = 0.035 ounce (oz)
(*See* also Appendix for metric conversion tables).

I have also tried to keep medical terms to the minimum. Some, however, are necessary. 'Acute' poisoning means taking a lethal dose all at once; in 'chronic' poisoning the victim is fed small doses which build up over days, weeks or months, until he or she dies. In the latter case, the poison must be cumulative – not all are. Chemical terms are unavoidable in any account of poisons, but, again, I have tried to use as few as possible and they have a lower-case letter. Trade names have a capital letter.

2 POISONS (LEGAL ASPECTS)

Poisoning is dealt with in England under the Offences Against the Person Act 1861, Section 23, which deals with causing death, grievous bodily harm or even annoyance by poisoning.

For a person to be convicted of murder by poison the jury must be convinced beyond reasonable doubt:
● 1. That the victim actually died of poisoning.
● 2. That the person accused actually administered the poison.
● 3. That the person accused intended to kill the victim.

These are not particularly easy things to prove, since few people will be able to give evidence as to how or why the murdered person received the poison, and most trials of this kind in Britain have therefore employed the best legal brains of the times. On the other hand, many poisonings are domestic affairs, or accomplished where the poisoner is in constant contact with the victim, such as in a hospital or nursing home. This makes the proving of the circumstances that much easier.

Other legal aspects include the ability to acquire poisons. Up until 1851 it was possible to buy arsenic and many other poisons over the counter without restriction. The Arsenic Act of that year restricted its sale and also the sale of other poisons. Anyone selling the poison had to record the sale in a book in a specified way. The purchaser, or a witness to the sale, had to be known to the seller. This set the pattern for all subsequent acts including those specifying who could actually sell poisons. In 1933 a Poisons Board was set up to advise the Secretary of State what poisons should be on the poisons list and in 1951 the Dangerous Drugs Act regulated the supply of addictive drugs such as heroin and cocaine. Later acts have restricted the sale of dangerous pesticides and herbicides.

Thus, the availability of poisons today is much less than it used to be and there are a great deal fewer cases of homicide by poisoning. This can sometimes work to the advantage of the potential poisoner, for today's general practitioner will have seen far fewer poisoning cases than his predecessors and there is a much greater chance that he will regard the symptoms of the victim as unfortunate but unsuspicious. In addition some poisons, such as arsenic, produce symptoms which are easily mistaken for other illnesses. Audrey Homan, after insuring the life of her eighteen-year-old daughter, in Alabama, in 1978 poisoned her with arsenic over a period of five months. Much of this time the teenager spent in various hospitals undergoing tests for an apparent wasting disease. (*See* also ARSENIC page 46).

2 POISONS FROM FUNGI

Availability	6/10
Effectiveness	7/10
Detectability	5/10

In Greek and Roman times the use of fungi was a relatively common method of murder. But today, accidental poisoning is about the only sort met with, and these are rare. In Britain there are not more than a dozen poisonous species among a total of over 3,500.

The most dangerous are the *Amanita* group, *Amanita verna* (Destroying Angel), *Amanita muscaria* (Fly Agaric), *Amanita pantherina* (Panther Cap) and *Amanita phalloides* (Death Cap). The latter is probably the most poisonous mushroom in the world. Even one mushroom can cause serious illness, and three (about 40g) are usually fatal. Death Cap is found in deciduous woods in autumn and, like other members of the group, contains a number of poisons of which amanitine is the most deadly.

EFFECTS
● The poisons are mostly slow acting and give rise to vomiting, diarrhoea and severe abdominal pain. Then follows a period without symptoms in which the patient thinks he has recovered, only to suffer subsequent renal and hepatic failure, hallucinations and finally death.
● Fly Agaric used to be used as a fly poison and contains muscarine, a powerful hallucinogen, which has been used for hundreds of years in religious and magical rituals. This is the 'magic mushroom' so beloved of the hippie cults in the 1960s.

Ergot is a parasitic fungus which grows on cereals and before the days of chemical crop spraying could be milled into the flour and cause serious illness and death to people who ate the contaminated bread. It contains another hallucinogen which is closely related to LSD.

EFFECTS
● Ingestion of ergot can lead to swelling and gangrene in the limbs and also causes contraction of the uterus and abortion. The amount needed to cause an abortion, however, is near the fatal dose.

REAL-LIFE EXAMPLES
● Greek dramatist Euripides describes a murder by mushrooms which occurred in 450 BC. Roman Emperor Claudius was poisoned by mushrooms, it is thought by his wife Agrippina, in AD54, to ensure that her son Nero succeeded to the title.

FICTIONAL EXAMPLES
● In the film *The Beguiled*, a seminary of young girls conspires to cook poisonous mushrooms in order to kill the interloper, Clint Eastwood.

2 POISONS FROM PLANTS: ACONITE

Availability	8/10
Effectiveness	8/10
Detectability	6/10

Aconite (Aconitum napellus) is a cottage-garden plant, which also grows wild all over Europe and North America. Known in addition as monkshood, wolfsbane and in Ireland as blue rocket, its leaves look something like parsley and its roots like horse radish. Both roots and leaves contain chemicals known as alkaloids, the principal one being aconitine, which is extremely poisonous. It is said that the lethal dose is about 1 mg and, if taken orally, the symptoms appear within eight minutes and death can occur within several hours. Large doses can kill almost immediately.

It has some medicinal uses, having been used as a liniment for conditions such as rheumatism and sciatica, since it can be absorbed through the skin and has at low concentrations a mildly anaesthetic property.

It is also one of the oldest of the poisons, being well known to the ancient Greeks and Romans. Indeed, so popular was it for getting rid of unwanted relatives, that the Emperor Trajan banned its cultivation in Roman gardens.

EFFECTS
- Aconite is absorbed through the gastro-intestinal tract and affects the central nervous system, paralysing the muscles. The first signs are a burning and tingling sensation in the mouth, numbness in the tongue, throat and face, followed by nausea, vomiting and blurred vision. Breathing is at first rapid then slows as the respiratory muscles become paralysed, but death usually occurs as a result of paralysis of the heart muscles.

REAL-LIFE EXAMPLES
- In 1882 Dr Lamson visited his brother-in-law, fifteen-year-old Percy, who suffered paralysis of the lower limbs at the latter's special school in Wimbledon. He gave him some Dundee cake and left quickly. The boy fell ill rapidly and died the same night. Suspicions were raised immediately because Lamson's wife stood to inherit from Percy's death, but the only test for the poison at the time was taste, a tingling sensation on the tongue. Nevertheless, Dr Lamson was convicted of murder and hanged.
- There is also a recorded case in America of a dentist who poisoned his father-in-law with aconite hidden in a filling. He died quickly in what was at first suspected to be a heart attack.

2 POISONS FROM PLANTS: BELLADONNA

Availability	3/10
Effectiveness	6/10
Detectability	7/10

Belladonna is a plant , whose scientific designation is *Atropa belladonna*. It gets its name from the Italian for 'beautiful woman', because women have for centuries past used an extract of the plant as eye drops, to widen the pupils and thus make them look more attractive. The plant is also called deadly nightshade. It is native to Europe, but has been transported as an ornamental plant to many parts of the world. It has pale purple-blue flowers from June to September, and purple-black berries.

All parts of the plant are poisonous, especially the berries, leaves and roots. Rabbits sometimes eat deadly nightshade and can pass on the effects to those who are unwise enough to consume meat from the animals.

The poisonous components are a group of chemicals called alkaloids and include atropine, hyoscyamine, hyoscine and belladonna. They paralyse the parasympathetic nervous system, which inhibits heart action and encourages digestive action, thus increasing the heart rate and inhibiting digestive action. Atropine also stimulates the central nervous system and gives rise to excitement and sometimes delirium. Belladonna is a constituent of cough mixtures for bronchitis and whooping cough because it helps to control coughing and dries up mucus.

EFFECTS

- The symptoms of belladonna poisoning are hot and dry skin and mouth, dilated pupils, increased heart rate – the heart beat can often be heard from some distance away – fever, convulsions and eventual death. The symptoms may, however, take several hours to develop and the patient may last for several days before dying.
- Lethal doses have been reported at less than 10 milligrams (mg) for a child and less than 100 mg for an adult.
- Stimulants such as atropine are sometimes injected to counteract the effects of aconite poisoning.
- Atropine is eliminated almost entirely by the kidneys and thus can be detected in the urine of a poisoned victim.

2 POISONS FROM PLANTS: CURARE

Availability	3/10
Effectiveness	7/10
Detectability	4/10

Curare is derived from certain South American jungle vines and widely used by the natives to tip their arrows, because it quickly paralyses and kills it victims. The principal ingredient is the alkaloid tubocurarine which, when isolated in the 1930s, passed into medical use as a muscle relaxant, to help keep patients still during delicate operations. 20–30 mg of the pure alkaloid produces a paralysis lasting 30 minutes, but, since it also paralyses the respiratory muscles, patients must be artificially ventilated. Today there are synthetic muscle relaxants which mimic the effect of curare. Examples are succinylcholine chloride and Pavulon, both of which have been used as murder weapons.

Crime writers will appreciate that the availability of these chemicals is largely restricted to hospitals and clinics, unless one is able to visit the steamy jungles of South America.

EFFECTS
- Curare and its synthetic equivalents all work by blocking the neurotransmitter acetyl choline, resulting in paralysis of the muscles. The poison has no effect if taken by mouth, but injection or intravenous administration cause paralysis starting with the eyelids and face and proceeding to the diaphragm within a matter of seconds. The pulse drops and death occurs rapidly due to paralysis of the lungs. During death throes, the victim turns blue. After death, the inflamed liver gives an indication of curare poisoning and, with care, spectroscopic analysis of the blood tissue can establish the presence of the poison. But succinylcholine chloride breaks down rapidly and is almost impossible to detect after death.

REAL-LIFE EXAMPLES
- In 1963, Dr Coppolino began an affair with a patient. The patient's husband died. Then the doctor's wife died. But instead of marrying his lover he married someone else and his lover went to the police. The doctor was accused of killing his patient by injecting succinylcholine chloride. He was found not guilty of killing his patient, but guilty of killing his wife.
- Two Filipino nurses were convicted in 1977 of poisoning patients in Ann Arbor hospital, Michigan, by adding Pavulon to their intravenous drips.

FICTIONAL EXAMPLES
- In a typical locked-room case Carter Dickson, in *Red Widow Murders*, has a murder victim with curare in his bloodstream but no puncture wound.
- Agatha Christie's *Death In The Clouds* gives us a body killed with a curare-laden dart propelled from a blowpipe. (Or was it?)

2 POISONS FROM PLANTS: DIGITALIS

Availability	8/10
Effectiveness	6/10
Detectability	8/10

The foxglove (*Digitalis purpurea*) is a tall plant, with purple to white flowers, which is found in many gardens and also grows wild in Europe and North America. Although all parts of the plant are poisonous the leaves are the most toxic, containing digitalis and two similar poisonous compounds, digoxin and digitoxin. It has been known since 1775 that an extract of dried foxglove leaves could cure dropsy, a condition where fluid accumulates under the skin or body cavities, but the extreme toxicity of the extract caused it to fall out of use until, in the 1920s, digitalis became the treatment for heart failure.

EFFECTS
- In very small amounts, digitalis strengthens each heartbeat and lengthens the rest periods. This increases blood flow and helps to get rid of fluids. In larger amounts, the heart beat becomes irregular and eventually stops altogether. Digitalis preparations taken by mouth cause headaches, nausea, vomiting and blurred vision, laboured breathing, convulsions and death.
- Only about 20 per cent of digitalis is absorbed by the gastro-intestinal track, whereas nearly all the digoxin and digitoxin are absorbed. This means that they have a smaller lethal dose, 5 to 25 mg, whereas for digitalis it may be several grams.

REAL-LIFE EXAMPLES
- In 1863 Dr Count de la Pommerais, a Paris homoeopathic physician, poisoned his mistress Madame de Pawr with digitalis. Suspicions were aroused because he had heavily insured her before her death. But at the time there was no reliable chemical test for the poison. Professor Tardieu, from Paris University, was able to show that extracts he made from the dead woman's organs and injected into dogs and frogs killed them with the same symptoms as Mme de Pawr. Pommerais was convicted of murder.

FICTIONAL EXAMPLES
- Agatha Christie, in *Appointment with Death* and in *Postern of Fate*, uses digitoxia (digitoxin) as the murder agent.
- *Unorthodox Practices* by Marissa Piesman has the victims killed with digitalis powder in food.

2 POISONS FROM PLANTS: HEMLOCK

Availability	7/10
Effectiveness	7/10
Detectability	6/10

Not a very common poison these days, though the hemlock plant (*Conium maculatum*) grows wild all over Europe and North America. It can grow up to six feet high and has small white flowers. Its leaves look a bit like parsley and could be used to make a salad. The leaves, fruits and root are poisonous, though it is said that the root is not poisonous during the spring. The plant contains a mixture of alkaloids of which the main one is coniine. A very poisonous chemical, the lethal dose is about 300-400 mg for an 11-stone person. Quail often eat hemlock seeds and seem to be immune to the poison, but poisoning can result from eating the contaminated flesh.

EFFECTS
- Hemlock poison is similar to curare in that it causes paralysis of the muscles, though the effect is somewhat slower, the first symptoms taking possibly half an hour to appear. Gradual weakening of muscle power is experienced, often with some pain in the muscles. The sight can be lost, although the mind remains clear until death, which usually occurs from paralysis of the lungs. It may take several hours for a victim to die. There is no antidote, but pumping out the stomach can work if it is done immediately the poison has been taken.
- As with curare, analysis of the liver, blood and tissue can establish the presence of coniine, but usually only specialised laboratories can do it.

REAL-LIFE EXAMPLES
- Perhaps the most famous is the death of Socrates in Athens in 399BC. Condemned to die for 'impiety' and 'corrupting the young' – encouraging them to think for themselves – he was forced to drink a cup of hemlock. According to his pupil Plato, Socrates walked about until his legs felt heavy then lay down on his bed and the paralysis gradually spread to his chest, when he died.

FICTIONAL EXAMPLE
- In Lia Metera's *Hidden Agenda* a lawyer dies from eating a salad containing hemlock leaves.

2 POISONS FROM PLANTS: HYOSCINE

Availability	7/10
Effectiveness	6/10
Detectability	7/10

Hyoscine is an alkaloid found in several plants. It occurs in the leaves and seeds of henbane (*Hyocyamus niger*) a botanical relative of the deadly nightshade (*see* BELLADONNA page 38) and is also found in thorn apple (sometimes called jimson weed) (*Datura stramonium*). Both henbane and thorn apple occasionally grow wild in southern Britain and can sometimes be found in gardens. Both plants grow to about two to three feet high. Henbane has hairy leaves, yellow bell-shaped flowers and a nauseous smell. Thorn apple has white or purple flowers, a prickly fruit and also an unpleasant odour. All parts of both plants are poisonous. And in North America where jimson weed is fairly common both adults and children have been poisoned by drinking tea made from the leaves of this plant.

Hyoscine is sometimes known as scopolamine and its effects are somewhat similar to atropine (*see* BELLADONNA) in that it depresses the central nervous system. Hyoscine is used medicinally in very small doses to relieve anxiety, stomach pains and travel sickness. In stronger doses it causes hallucinations and impairs judgement and for this reason has been used as a 'truth drug'. It is rapidly absorbed through the mucous membranes and also the skin, but its action on the body is not fully understood and individual reactions to the drug vary a great deal. This makes it uncertain as a medicine or a poison. The lethal dose is taken to be 10 to 40 mg.

EFFECTS
- The effects, which can take several hours to appear, include headache, vertigo, extreme thirst and dry sensation of the skin.
- The pupils of the eye often dilate and this can occur if the eyes are rubbed after handling the leaves of the plants. Blurred vision often occurs and sometimes blindness.
- Drowsiness and a weak pulse eventually take over leading to coma and death.
- Hyoscine can be detected and measured in the body, usually in the liver, a considerable time after death, even after dismembering and burying the body, as Dr Crippen discovered to his cost.

REAL-LIFE EXAMPLES
- In one of the most famous murders, probably the most famous poisoning of all time, which occurred in 1910, Dr Crippen murdered his wife with hyoscine.

FICTIONAL EXAMPLE
- Jimson weed is used in *Over The Edge* by Jonathan Kellerman to cause the mental collapse of one of the characters.

2 POISONS FROM PLANTS: RICIN

Availability	3/10
Effectiveness	8/10
Detectability	2/10

Ricin is obtained from the seeds or beans of the castor-oil plant (*Ricinus communis*). This occurs naturally in Africa and India and parts of North America, where it is often grown as an ornamental plant, and it can be cultivated elsewhere in a greenhouse. Castor-oil is obtained commercially from the beans by extraction and the ricin removed by steam distillation, a process which can easily be done in most school chemical laboratories.

Ricin is one of the most toxic substances known. It has been estimated that a gram, about enough to cover your little finger nail, is enough to kill 36,000 people (the whole population of a small town). About six beans contain enough poison to be fatal, but it must be released, by grinding up the beans in a pestle and mortar, for example. Swallowing the beans whole would probably be ineffective since the hard seed-coat prevents absorption of the poison.

EFFECTS
● Taken orally, Ricin causes a burning sensation in the mouth, so it would need to be disguised by some hot, strong-tasting food, such as coffee or a curry.
● The poison causes nausea, cramps and drowsiness. Its effect is to cause clumping together of the red blood corpuscles, which leads to circulatory collapse, blood in the urine and stools, convulsions, coma and death. But symptoms take from several hours to days to develop and death may occur up to twelve days after taking a lethal dose.
● Ricin is extremely difficult to detect in the body. Tell-tale signs are an extremely high white blood count. Death from ricin poisoning has in the past been attributed to toxaemia (blood poisoning).

REAL-LIFE EXAMPLE
● In 1978, Georgi Markov, a defector from Communist Bulgaria who worked for the BBC in London making broadcasts to his own country, was waiting for a bus on Waterloo Bridge. He felt a sharp pain in the back of his thigh and turned to see a man picking up an umbrella. The man quickly disappeared in the crowds. Later that night Markov began running a high temperature and died in hospital four days later. A post-mortem revealed, embedded in his thigh, a steel pellet only 1.5mm in diameter which had contained ricin. Markov's wife believed the Bulgarian secret service to be responsible.

2 POISONS FROM PLANTS: STRYCHNINE

Availability	5/10
Effectiveness	8/10
Detectability	8/10

The shrub *Strychinos nux vomica* grows in India and other tropical countries including Hawaii. The berries, which are usually dried and powdered, contain the alkaloid strychnine and the powder has been known since at least the 17th century as a method of poisoning vermin. Before the existence of a reliable test it was also one of the most common homicidal poisons. Strychnine has an extremely bitter taste and various methods have been used to disguise it, such as brandy, coffee, hot chocolate and jam. In very low concentrations it has been used medicinally as a nerve stimulant and as a 'tonic' to improve the appetite of convalescent patients. The lethal dose is usually taken to be about 100mg, but amounts as low as 10mg have been known to kill.

EFFECTS
- These are well-known and undisguisable. The prosecution summed them up in the trial of Ethel Major for poisoning her husband, when the defence claimed that even though the man had two doses of the drug it was still suicide. 'No-one except a madman,' said prosecutor O'Sullivan, 'having taken one dose and experienced its effects, would take another'.
- The symptoms may arise in ten to twenty minutes, longer if taken on a full stomach. Since strychnine attacks the central nervous system it causes all the muscles of the body to contract together, causing extremely painful convulsions, which occur every ten to fifteen minutes. The spasms increase in intensity until the victim is almost continuously in an arched-back position, called opisthotonus, with only the back of the head and the heels touching the floor. Asphyxiation, due to paralysis of the respiratory muscles, may cause death or the heart may fail.
- There are now reliable tests for strychnine which can be detected and estimated in the urine, organs or tissues of the body.

REAL-LIFE EXAMPLES
- There are many well-known cases of strychnine poisoning.
- Dr William Palmer, the Rugeley poisoner (1856), used it and so did Dr Neill Cream, who poisoned prostitutes in London in (1891).
- Eva Rablen poisoned her husband in Tuttletown, California, in 1929 and Ethel Major gave it to her spouse in a Lincolnshire village in 1934.

FICTIONAL EXAMPLES
- Agatha Christie had her murderer administer the poison in her first novel, *The Mysterious Affair At Styles*, disguising the taste with the victim's hot chocolate, and she used the same poison to dispatch Mr Appleton in *The Mysterious Mr Quinn*.

2 POISONS (INDUSTRIAL): ANTIMONY

Availability	8/10
Effectiveness	6/10
Detectability	8/10

Antimony is a bluish-white element similar to ARSENIC (*see* page 46). In its compounds (the element combined with other elements) it is extremely poisonous. Antimony was one of the components of ancient bronze and its compounds have been used as an eye cosmetic, to darken the skin around the eyes, and as an emetic, since Egyptian times. In an alloy with other metals the Romans fashioned it into small cups which would be filled with wine. When a feasting Roman could eat no more he would drink from the cup, vomit, and carry on eating. Its modern uses are in insecticides, paint, glass and rubber so it's available on industrial sites, etc. Antimony compounds can also be bought at a pharmacist, as poisoner Graham Young discovered, but a poison book has to be signed.

EFFECTS
- Antimony is like arsenic in that it produces nausea, frequent vomiting and severe diarrhoea, which are also symptoms of gastric fever (for which the poisoning was often mistaken). But, unlike with arsenic, antimony victims have a marked tendency to vomit up the poison and thus reduce its effectiveness. In fact, in Victorian times the most common antimony compound met with was antimony potassium tartrate, called 'tartar emetic'. This property of antimony compounds makes it very difficult to predict a lethal dose and in fact most poisoners have used it in small doses over a period, when they hoped the symptoms would be confused with gastric fever.
- Lethal doses have been quoted as 50mg to 100mg, but people have survived much larger doses than this. The victims may last for hours or even several days before death intervenes, which will be due to circulatory or respiratory failure.
- Autopsy findings will show damage to the liver and other organs, and the gastro-intestinal tract may show congestion and swelling. The old test for antimony was the same as that for arsenic – Marsh's test, but modern instrumental techniques can distinguish between the two.

REAL-LIFE EXAMPLES
- In 1962, Graham Young was convicted of poisoning his father, sister and a school friend. He was just fifteen. Luckily, they all survived, but he was committed to Broadmoor, the hospital for the criminally insane. He then confessed that he had killed his step-mother, poisoning her with antimony. He was never charged with this offence. When he was released from Broadmoor, some ten years later, he was found a job with a chemical firm. He then killed two of his workmates with Thallium (*see* page 51) and severely injured four more, before he was finally convicted of murder and given life imprisonment.

2 POISONS (INDUSTRIAL: ARSENIC

Availability	7/10
Effectiveness	7/10
Detectability	8/10

Arsenic is an element and, like ANTIMONY (*see* page 45), in the elemental state is hardly absorbed by the body and therefore not poisonous. But arsenic *compounds* are lethal. The simplest, arsenic trioxide (white arsenic), resembles sugar, is almost tasteless and though not very soluble in water, in terms of use has been the most deadly and the classic poison for probably thousands of years. Certainly the Romans knew of it and it was favoured by Medieval and Renaissance poisoners, particularly as at the time there was no reliable test for it.

Arsenic compounds have been used medicinally for many years and today they are found in insecticides and herbicides, in textiles, paints and the making of certain types of glass. An arsenic-containing dye, Scheele's Green, was a common ingredient of wallpapers and paints and it was suggested that Napoleon, who may have died from arsenic poisoning, absorbed the poison from his wallpaper!

EFFECTS
- The action of arsenic (and antimony) on the body is not fully understood, but they may interfere with the function of certain vital enzymes. The symptoms of arsenic poisoning are similar to those of antimony poisoning. They usually appear within half an hour of administration and, with lethal doses, death can occur after a few hours. The best known antidote is dimercaprol, delivered by intramuscular injection.
- One of the advantages to the poisoner is that arsenic is cumulative, small doses being stored in the heart, lungs, liver and kidneys.
- Arsenic is also laid down in the hair, nails and teeth and this makes it easy to detect and estimate in the body. The study of the hair for example by modern techniques of analysis can reveal the pattern of administration and even the size of the doses given. The lethal dose is similar to antimony, about 50mg to 100mg.
- The human body can build up a tolerance to arsenic. As late as the early years of the twentieth century, peasants in the Austrian province of Styria took small doses with their food to improve their complexions and figures and because they thought it gave them extra strength climbing the mountains. It is thought that they could ingest well over the lethal dose without harm.

REAL-LIFE EXAMPLES
- Audrey Homan poisoned her husband with arsenic for the insurance, then tried to do the same with her teenaged daughter. She was convicted in Alabama in 1983. (*see* also POISONS (LEGAL ASPECTS) page 35).

FICTIONAL EXAMPLES
- One of the most ingenious uses of arsenic was that employed by Dorothy L. Sayers in her novel *Strong Poison*.

2 POISONS (INDUSTRIAL): CARBON MONOXIDE

Availability	8/10
Effectiveness	7/10
Detectability	8/10

This a colourless, odourless gas, which is formed from the incomplete combustion of carbon materials. Car exhausts contain 4–7 per cent carbon monoxide and a 1.4 litre car engine running in a small closed garage will generate a lethal level of the gas in about five minutes. Faulty gas heaters are another source and a number of accidental deaths occur every year by the use of these appliances in unventilated rooms.

EFFECTS
- Carbon monoxide works by replacing the oxygen in the haemoglobin molecule and thus prevents oxygen being transported in the blood. Death is by oxygen starvation, a kind of internal suffocation. The great danger with the gas is that it can work slowly and insidiously. As the concentration builds up the victim feels drowsy without knowing why, as he cannot smell the gas.
- A slight headache will be experienced with shortness of breath and, as the concentration increases these will get worse, being followed by nausea, chest pain and unconsciousness. A 0.1 per cent concentration of carbon monoxide in the air breathed will cause death in three hours.
- The only antidote is to remove from the source of the gas and administer oxygen. Artificial respiration in the open air may be necessary.
- Post-mortem changes include microscopic haemorrhages in the eyes and elsewhere, congestion and swelling of the brain, liver, and kidneys and spleen. The blood may also be cherry-red.

REAL-LIFE EXAMPLES
- Most murders come from the time when household gas contained carbon monoxide. Bath resident Reginald Hinks killed his father-in-law by putting the old man's head in the gas oven, in 1933. But he forgot that the bruise the victim sustained, being rendered unconscious first, would show up.
- In 1981, Ian Smith, a lecturer in physics in Leeds, killed his wife by exposing her, when she was asleep in a holiday caravan to pure carbon monoxide gas from a cylinder he stole from his college laboratory. But the level of the gas in his own blood was very low compared with his wife's so that his story of accidental poisoning was disproved.

FICTIONAL EXAMPLES
- In *Saturday The Rabbi Went Hungry*, Harry Kellerman has his fictional victim pass out with drink and the villain then puts him in a garage with the car engine running.
- In Robin Cook's *Coma* carbon monoxide is fed down the oxygen line during an operation, thus ensuring the collapse and death of a patient.

2 POISONS (INDUSTRIAL) CYANIDE

Availability	8/10
Effectiveness	9/10
Detectability	8/10

Hydrogen cyanide, sometimes called hydrocyanic acid or prussic acid, is a gas. If breathed in its action is immediate and it can cause death within minutes. The salts, sodium cyanide and potassium cyanide are solids and not poisonous when dry, but rapidly change to the gas in the presence of slightly acid water. Thus when ingested by mouth, injected or even coming into contact with moist skin they release the deadly gas which is quickly absorbed by the body.

Cyanides are found in the seeds of apples, pears, plums, peaches, apricots, cherries and almonds. They are also present in laurel leaves. Soaking laurel leaves and evaporating the extract gives a lethal dose of the poison.

Potassium cyanide is used to case harden steel, in photography and electroplating and to extract gold and silver from their ores. It was also used as an 'exit pill', by Nazi leaders after the Second World War and by many spies. Sodium cyanide pellets are dropped into acids to produce hydrogen cyanide in some American prison execution chambers.

EFFECTS
● Hydrogen cyanide prevents the body's red blood cells from absorbing oxygen and subsequent death has been called 'internal asphyxiation'. Initial symptoms include rapid respiration, gasping for breath, dizziness and headache, vomiting and unconsciousness.
● Convulsion usually precedes death, which can take place any time up to about four hours. A lethal dose is about 200mg to 300mg.
● The well-known bitter-almond smell can sometimes be detected near the mouth of a victim and more commonly in the stomach, but not everyone is capable of detecting the smell and it is also characteristic of other, non-poisonous, compounds. Better indicators are the blue colouration of the face and lips and the cherry-red appearance of the blood, although this is also shown in poisoning by CARBON MONOXIDE (*see* page 47).
● Surprisingly enough there are antidotes, if they can be administered quickly enough. Amyl nitrite is first given and oxygen to help the heart. Then sodium nitrite followed by sodium thiosulphate is injected intravenously.

REAL-LIFE EXAMPLES
● Seattle housewife Stella Nickell substituted cyanide for the contents of her husband's headache capsules in 1986.

FICTIONAL EXAMPLES
● Isaac Asimov's killer used hydrogen cyanide gas in *Whiff Of Death*.
● In *Sudden Death*, William Kienzle's villain places cyanide in his victim's shampoo bottle.

2 POISONS (INDUSTRIAL): MERCURY

Availability	6/10
Effectiveness	7/10
Detectability	8/10

The element mercury is the only metal which is liquid at room temperature. The thick silver liquid used to fascinate school children who delighted in putting their fingers in it. But although the liquid is not very harmful, the vapour is poisonous and you get a surprising amount of it above the liquid, so this experiment is no longer done in schools. Mercury compounds, especially those soluble in a water, are also very poisonous, although mercury salts in low concentrations have been used medicinally for hundreds of years. One of the treatments for syphilis, since the sixteenth century, has been mercury salts. Mercurous chloride (calomel) used to be a recommended laxative for children and mercuric chloride (corrosive sublimate) has antiseptic and antibacterial properties. Barometers, thermometers, mirrors and dental amalgams have all incorporated mercury. And the previous use of mercury compounds in fur-processing and hat manufacture led to the expression 'mad as a hatter', since mercury poisoning can give symptoms not unlike drunkenness and insanity.

EFFECTS

● Taken by mouth mercury salts have a strong metallic taste which needs to be disguised. Their corrosive action causes the mouth and throat to become painful. Vomiting usually takes place after about fifteen minutes and abdominal pain is experienced together with diarrhoea and muscle cramps. The kidneys are damaged and ulceration of the bowel may occur.

● Inflammation of the mouth causes the teeth to become loose and a characteristic blue-black line may be seen on the gums. The lethal dose is about two grams of mercuric chloride taken by mouth or about 100mg injected intravenously.

● Exposure to mercury vapour damages the central nervous system and causes a characteristic psychosis which has in the past led to suicide.

REAL-LIFE EXAMPLES

● Roland B. Molineux supposedly poisoned two members of the Knickerbocker Athletic Club of New York in 1889, by anonymously sending through the post mercuric cyanide mixed with Bromo-Seltzer crystals. He was first convicted of the murders but at a subsequent trial acquitted.

● Homosexual poet Sir Thomas Overbury was thrown into the Tower of London in 1613, when his former lover Robert Carr took Lady Francis Howard as his mistress. Overbury was then fed mercury salts and other poisons over a period of months, until he died, to make it look as if he had succumbed to the damp conditions in the Tower.

2 POISONS (INDUSTRIAL): PHOSPHORUS

Availability	8/10
Effectiveness	6/10
Detectability	8/10

Phosphorus is a non-metallic element, a waxy solid which comes in two forms: yellow and red. Red phosphorus is pretty inert and not toxic, but yellow phosphorus is a very dangerous material indeed. When dry it will burst into flames in the air and it is normally kept under water or oil. It also glows in the dark. Yellow phosphorus is extremely toxic and used to be a common constituent of rat poison and match heads. But the slow absorption of the poison among match workers led to necrosis of the jaw, called 'Phossy jaw', in which the bone crumbled away. Today match heads do not contain it, although rat poisons may contain phosphorus compounds. They are also used in the manufacture of explosives and pyrotechnic products. Chronic phosphorus poisoning (absorption of small amounts over long period) is difficult to detect, since phosphorus compounds occur in the body.

EFFECTS
- Phosphorus is absorbed by the gastro-intestinal tract where it passes to other organs and can do particular damage to the liver.
- Symptoms include a garlic smell on the breath, burning pains in the stomach, vomiting (the vomit and excretion glow in the dark), convulsion and coma. The symptoms may then appear to subside, only to reappear a day or two later, leading to jaundice, collapse and eventual death, which may take several days or even one or two weeks.
- The lethal dose of the element is only some 65mg, but in compounds larger doses will be necessary.
- The autopsy will show jaundice, necrosis of the liver, kidney and heart and haemorrhages in the intestinal tract. Many of the organs will have the characteristic garlic odour. Large concentrations of phosphorus can be detected in the blood and organs, but low concentrations might be missed.

REAL-LIFE EXAMPLES
- 66-year-old Mary Wilson, the widow of Windy Nook, as she was called, was convicted in 1959 of the murders of two husbands by giving them rat poison, but it was surmised that she had killed at least two more by the same method.
- In 1953 Louisa Merryfield poisoned an elderly widow, to whom she was a companion, with phosphorus, in rat poison, and was hanged.

2 POISONS (INDUSTRIAL): THALLIUM

Availability	5/10
Effectiveness	9/10
Detectability	6/10

Thallium is a metallic element, similar chemically to lead and mercury, and considerably more poisonous than either. It was only discovered in the last century and has some claim to be the perfect poison. Its salts, like the sulphate and acetate, are soluble in water, so they can easily be given in tea, coffee, etc. They are almost tasteless and the symptoms of thallium poisoning are easily confused with other illnesses like influenza, peripheral neuritis, typhus and encephalitis. The only drawback is that many preparations containing thallium salts, such as ant-bait, rat poisons, and pesticides are no longer sold in many European countries and the USA because they are so poisonous, although they are available in some developing countries. Thallium salts may be obtained, from some pharmacies, by signing a poisons book. They are also used in the manufacture of some dyes, paints and glass.

EFFECTS
- The action of thallium salts is not fully understood, but they are thought to affect the nerve cells and upset the calcium balance. This causes disorders similar to influenza.
- A lethal dose, about 800mg of thallium sulphate, causes death in 20 to 40 hours, but, like arsenic, thallium is cumulative and repeated small doses cause inflammation of the nerves to the hands and feet, facial paralysis and loss of hair. Before it was recognised as being so poisonous it was used as a depilatory for women.
- Thallium is retained in the body and, like arsenic, can be detected in the hair. It is probably the only poison which has been found in the ashes of a body after cremation.

REAL-LIFE EXAMPLES
- In 1972 Graham Young was convicted of murdering two of his work colleagues with thallium salts and attempting to murder several more. He put the poison in their tea.
- Martha Lowenstein was tried in 1938, in Vienna, for poisoning an elderly relative, a lodger, her husband and her baby, with thallium. She was convicted and beheaded.
- In 1947, 62-year-old Australian, Caroline Grills, began adding rat poison containing thallium to people's tea. She killed four people before being caught literally in the act. She became known in prison as 'Aunt Thally'.

FICTIONAL EXAMPLES
- Ngaio Marsh featured thallium in *The Final Curtain* in 1947, but her account of its effects is full of inaccuracies.
- Agatha Christie's *The Pale Horse* (1961) on the other hand, was hailed as the best description of thallium poisoning found outside a text-book.

2 POISONS (MEDICAL): CANTHARIDIN

Availability	3/10
Effectiveness	5/10
Detectability	6/10

Cantharides is a powder made from the dried wings and body cases of the beetle *Cantharis vesicatoria,* which is found in Italy, Southern Russia and Spain. It is sometimes known as Spanish Fly. The active agent in the powder is cantharidin. It used to be used as a blistering agent when applied to skin as a plaster and was intended to counteract severe pains such as sciatica or to encourage the absorption of fluid in thickened joints. It has also been used in dilute solution to stimulate the scalp.

It has an unjustified reputation as an aphrodisiac and there are many recorded cases of it having been given to women to stimulate them sexually, usually with disastrous and sometimes fatal results.

EFFECTS
- Cantharidin is an irritant to all cells and tissues and, if a dose is taken orally it will produce blistering of the mouth, nausea, vomiting, stomach pains and bloody diarrhoea. When it passes out of the urinary system it irritates the genitals and this may have given rise to the idea that it was an aphrodisiac. But it is highly dangerous and produces a severe fall in blood pressure and eventual death due to respiratory failure.
- The lethal dose is considered to be 60mg of cantharidin or 160-170 mg of Spanish Fly powder.
- Autopsy findings are necrosis of many internal mucous membranes and concentrations of blood in the urinary organs.

REAL-LIFE EXAMPLES
- Arthur Ford was the manager of a wholesale chemist's business in London in 1954, although he was no chemist. He discovered that cantharidin was kept in the stores, but the chief chemist refused to let him have any explaining that it was a listed poison. Ford then stole some and fed it to two girls in the office on a bar of coconut ice. He also took some himself. All three were soon ill. He survived, but the two girls died 24 hours later in hospital. When the post-mortems revealed cantharidin poisoning he confessed.

FICTIONAL EXAMPLES
- In Jennie Melville's *Death In The Garden* a poisoning is effected by putting cantharidin in a whisky decanter.

2 POISONS (MEDICAL): CHLOROFORM

Availability	6/10
Effectiveness	5/10
Detectability	8/10

A volatile liquid, at one time chloroform was employed extensively by the medical profession to ease the pains of childbirth and also as a general anaesthetic for surgery. Little used today, chloroform occasionally appears in cough mixtures where its anaesthetic properties can help to soothe the bronchial passages. It is still readily available, however, as a solvent and bottles of it can often be found on shelves above work benches in many general chemical laboratories, and even school laboratories.

A colourless liquid, it has a very characteristic smell, which can usually be detected during the post-mortem examination of dead bodies which have been poisoned with chloroform. And its presence can be confirmed easily by chemical or spectroscopic tests.

EFFECTS
- Chloroform can be given by causing someone to inhale the vapour, for example by soaking a pad with the liquid then placing it over the victims nose. But if the liquid comes into contact with the skin it can cause blisters. And blisters can also occur in the mouth and oesophagus during administration of the liquid by mouth.
- Initially, the drug gives rise to pleasant feelings and it has been used for solvent sniffing, but it soon produces unconsciousness. Acting on the central nervous system it leads to respiratory failure and, if the victim does not die of this, death may take place several days later due to subsequent liver damage.
- The lethal dose has been quoted as 10 to 15ml of the liquid, although recovery has been recorded from doses as high as 150ml.

REAL-LIFE EXAMPLES
- John Wayne Gacy, the Chicago area serial killer, often used chloroform to render his victims unconscious and may even have murdered some in this way.
- Dot King, a New York model, was chloroformed in her apartment in 1923 during a robbery, and afterwards died. The killer was never found.
- Perhaps the most famous chloroform poisoning is the Adelaide Bartlett case. Edwin Bartlett died in December 1885, in Pimlico, and, during the post-mortem, it was found that his stomach contained chloroform. But medical opinion was divided on how it got there. Adelaide Bartlett was tried for murder, but the jury could not decide if Bartlett had taken it himself or if Adelaide had given it to him. She was acquitted.

2 POISONS (MEDICAL): INSULIN

Availability 6/10
Effectiveness 5/10
Detectability 2/10

Insulin is actually made in the pancreas and controls the amount of glucose (the product of carbohydrate digestion and sometimes erroneously called sugar) circulating in the blood. It enables muscles and other tissues to use glucose for energy-producing purposes. If the pancreas fails to produce insulin or doesn't produce enough, glucose levels rise in the bloodstream and it is excreted in the urine. This condition is known as diabetes mellitus and if untreated it will be fatal. Treatment is by injecting a solution of insulin under the skin (subcutaneously). The insulin can be derived from the pancreas of pigs or cattle, or these days genetically engineered human insulin can be produced. Daily or twice-daily injections keep diabetes sufferers alive. The amount of insulin must be carefully controlled.

The injection of a large dose of insulin is a method of murder, though access would be required to samples of insulin and the ability and opportunity to inject a victim with the drug.

In addition, since insulin already circulates in the body a large dose is not very easy to detect and might be missed, especially if death could be ascribed to other causes.

EFFECTS
- If too much insulin is injected the level of glucose in the blood falls and a condition known as hypoglycaemia or 'insulin shock' results. This is characterised by fatigue, reddening of the face, hunger, rapid heartbeat, shallow breathing, coma and eventually death.

REAL-LIFE EXAMPLE
- Ken Barlow, who was a male nurse in Huddersfield, called a doctor one night in May 1957, saying that his wife had collapsed and drowned in the bath at home. An autopsy showed that she had drowned, but two syringes were found in the kitchen. Minute examination of the body with a hand lens eventually showed two injection marks on the buttocks. Evidence was given at his trial that Barlow had boasted to colleagues that insulin injection would be the perfect murder method. And a biochemist reported that an extract from the tissues from Mrs Barlow's buttocks and injected into mice, produced all the symptoms of insulin overdose. He estimated by this means that there was a very large excess of insulin in the body. Barlow was convicted of murder.
- Nurse Beverley Allitt was convicted of murdering four young children in the children's ward at Grantham hospital in 1991 and trying to murder six more. Modern analytical methods were able to show that several children had extremely high levels of insulin in their bloodstreams, though she had also used other methods of murder as well.

2 POISONS (MEDICAL): MORPHINE AND CODEINE

Availability	6/10
Effectiveness	6/10
Detectability	7/10

Morphine and codeine are both alkaloids found in opium, the dried juice of the white Indian poppy, *Papapaver somniferum*. Opium itself had been in use for many years as a painkiller, but in the early 1800s morphine was isolated from it and proved to be a much more potent drug. A derivative, morphine hydrochloride, (often called 'morphia') is even more effective as it is soluble in water and easily given as a liquid or injected. Care must be taken in administering the drug as it is addictive and patients require larger and larger doses to get the same effect.

Codeine today is used as a sedative and painkiller and is found in combination with many other drugs including aspirin and caffeine. It too is addictive.

EFFECTS
- Both these drugs are called narcotic analgesics and are used medically in the control of severe pain. They work by depressing the central nervous system.
- After ingestion of a lethal dose, 300mg to 400mg, by mouth or injection, unconsciousness soon comes, with shallow breathing, cyanosis (bluish-purple discolouration of the skin), weak pulse and low blood pressure.
- Spasms of the gastro-intestinal tract and vomiting may occur and the characteristic condition of pinpoint pupils, which has tripped up many murderers, is seen.
- Convulsions may accompany codeine poisoning and coma and death from respiratory failure takes place with both drugs within six to twelve hours after ingestion. Morphine increases the effects of sedatives, analgesics and tranquillisers and if mixed with alcohol it works faster.

REAL-LIFE EXAMPLES
- Morphine has been method of choice for murder for many doctors. Edme Castaing (Paris physician, 1823), Carlyle Harris (New York medical student, 1891), Dr Robert Buchanan, (New York, 1892) and Dr Robert Clements, who in 1947, in Southport, committed suicide (by taking morphine) after police became suspicious when his fourth wife died (of morphine poisoning).

FICTIONAL EXAMPLES
- Agatha Christie has made use of this drug as a poison, in *By The Pricking Of My Thumbs*, *Sad Cypress*, and *There Is A Tide*.

2 POISONS (MEDICAL): SLEEPING PILLS I

Availability	6/10
Effectiveness	7/10
Detectability	8/10

Chloral hydrate is the oldest of the sleeping drugs, but it has an unpleasant taste and much more powerful drugs are now on the market so it is little used today. The drug is soluble in water and could be added to a drink (the so-called knock-out drops) and often proved a lethal combination with alcohol. Popularly known, in the first half of the century, as a 'Micky Finn' the combination was often used by the criminal fraternity to render a victim unconscious so that he could be robbed, kidnapped, or killed.

EFFECTS
● The drug affects the central nervous system. Symptoms take about half an hour to appear and include sleepiness and mental confusion, followed by coma, the duration of which depends on the amount taken.
● Death may take several hours to occur and results from pneumonia or respiratory failure. But the lethal dose can be as high as several grams.

A more modern class of substances used to produce sleep are the benzodiazepines. They are also used as tranquillisers and include Valium and Librium. Examples of those that are used specifically to produce sleep are Mogadon and Dalinane.

EFFECTS
● Benzodiazepines are similar in effect to chloral hydrate, and are even more dangerous when taken with alcohol.
● Most of these drugs can be detected in the blood up to about 24 hours after ingesting them and often up to 120 hours in the urine.

REAL-LIFE EXAMPLES
● Charlie Parton, a London petty criminal in 1889, fed a businessman chloral hydrate in order to rob him. But the man died and Charlie was hanged.
● San Francisco gang leader Juanita Spinelli gave the drug to an associate suspected of betraying them and when he was unconscious had him thrown into the Sacramento River. In November 1941 she became the first woman to be executed in California.

FICTIONAL EXAMPLES
● Chloral hydrate appears in Agatha Christie's *Secret Adversary* and *The Clocks* as a lethal poison and in *Ten Little Niggers* to render Emily Brent unconscious, when she was injected with CYANIDE (*see* page 48).

2 POISONS (MEDICAL): SLEEPING PILLS II

Availability	8/10
Effectiveness	6/10
Detectability	6/10

Today probably the commonest drugs used in sleeping pills are the barbiturates. Since the 1950s their ready availability on prescription has led to their becoming the most usual method of suicide, if not murder. There have literally been hundreds of these drugs introduced over the years and they are usually divided into four types depending on their speed of action.

Long-acting
Act up to twelve to twenty four hours. These are broken down slowly in the body and may be excreted partly unchanged in the urine. Examples are Veronal and Luminal. Lethal dose 1–4g.

Intermediate-acting
Act for up to eight hours and only a small portion is excreted unchanged. Soneryl and Amytal are examples. A dangerous dose is 1–2g.

Short-acting
Nembutal is an example. This is lethal at about 1g.

Ultra-short-acting
Sodium thiopentone is one. These are injected for the production of anaesthesia during operations. It has been reported that in America these are the most widely used drugs for suicide among doctors.

EFFECTS
- Barbiturates all depress the central nervous system causing sleep or anaesthesia and in large doses produce coma which may last from one to several days. This is followed by kidney failure, respiratory failure and death.
- The effects are increased if alcohol is taken at the same time and patients suffering from acute hepatitis (liver damage) also develop the effects sooner and the lethal dose could be much lower.
- Evidence of barbiturate poisoning will be shown in the body by oedema (excess of water in the body), froth and pus in the lungs and congestion of the brain. The drug used may often be detected in the urine.

REAL-LIFE EXAMPLES
- Dr Arthur Waite, from New York, used Veronal on his in-laws in 1916.
- John Armstrong was a sick-berth attendant at the Royal Naval Hospital in Gosport in 1955 when his five-month-old son died. He said that the child had eaten poisonous red berries, but the red material in the child's stomach turned out to be the coating of Seconal capsules. He was convicted of murder.

2 POISONS (PESTICIDES): NICOTINE

Availability	9/10
Effectiveness	8/10
Detectability	7/10

This alkaloid was first isolated from the tobacco plant *Nicotiana tabacum* in 1829. A dangerously strong solution of the toxin is easily obtained by simply soaking cigarette or cigar butts in water and evaporating the extract. The alkaloid itself is a pale yellow liquid which oxidises in the air to a brown sticky mass. It was formerly extensively employed as an horticultural spray, but is much less used today because of its high toxicity and the number of fatal accidents occurring to people who use it.

EFFECTS
- Nicotine can be rapidly absorbed by the skin or the gastrointestinal tract, injected or inhaled and even spillage into the eyes can be dangerous. It works by stimulating then depressing the central nervous system.
- Muscles, including those in the diaphragm, are paralysed and death occurs by respiratory failure. Its speed of action is exceeded by few toxins except CYANIDE (*see* page 48).
- A lethal dose is 40mg to 60mg and death can occur within minutes and rarely more than four hours after this amount has been ingested.
- Symptoms of nicotine poisoning include an initial burning sensation in the mouth, throat and stomach, followed by nausea, vomiting, diarrhoea, convulsions, coma and death.
- Smokers only usually absorb enough of the drug to become slightly stimulated, though they will have a higher tolerance to the poison.
- Activated charcoal may be given as an antidote, and atropine (*see* also BELLADONNA, page 38 and HYOSCINE, page 42) has also been used.

REAL-LIFE EXAMPLES
- The Belgian Comte Hippolyte de Bocarme was one of the first to use the poison, in 1850, to get rid of his wife's brother and inherit her fortune. The case was the spur for the first proper extraction and chemical analysis of the poison from bodily fluids, and was made by Jean Stas, Professor of Chemistry at the Ecole Royale Militaire in Brussels. The Comte went to the guillotine.

FICTIONAL EXAMPLES
- Charlotte MacLeod used nicotine in her novel *Bilbao Looking Glass* to kill the victim, the poison being placed in a Martini.
- The dentist murderer in *Poison* by Ed McBain put nicotine in a bottle of Scotch and to kill another victim placed the poison in a temporary crown with a thin spot so it would be worn away easily by brushing or eating.

2 POISONS (PESTICIDES): PARAQUAT

Availability	8/10
Effectiveness	6/10
Detectability	7/10

This is a widely used contact herbicide both for agricultural and horticultural use. Its advantage to gardeners is that it is inactivated by clay particles in the soil. Water soluble, it can be bought in solid form (Weedol) and dissolved, but care must be taken using the solution to avoid skin and eye contact as paraquat poisons by ingestion, inhalation or absorption through the skin. Weedkiller preparations these days often contain diquat which is only half as toxic as paraquat and therefore requires twice as much to achieve the same poisoning effect.

EFFECTS
- A fairly large dose of paraquat applied to the skin causes severe irritation and, if taken orally, often causes burning of the mouth and throat, but the effects may be slow to develop, sometimes not appearing for two or three days. Liver and kidney damage can occur and this will eventually result in death.
- Smaller doses can still be fatal as paraquat causes fibrosis of the lungs making breathing difficult and death will subsequently take place, though this can take several weeks. A fifth of a pint (about 100ml) of a 20 per cent solution of paraquat once killed a man in seven days and about a quarter of this took fifteen days to kill another man.
- Even though the toxin takes a long time to work there is no real antidote and the only treatment is to try and relieve the symptoms.
- Paraquat and its relatives are not difficult to detect in the body, one of its effects being that it turns the victim's urine blue.

REAL-LIFE EXAMPLES
- Susan Barber, who lived in Southend in 1981, was fed up with her husband. He'd beaten her when he discovered her in bed with another man. So she put some weedkiller she found in the garden shed in his steak-and-kidney pie. It was Gramoxone, a concentrated solution of paraquat in water, which is not now available. He suffered headaches and a sore throat and the police believe she dosed the medicine he received for this as well. He died 20 days later in Hammersmith Hospital. Susan was convicted of murder.

2 POISONS (PESTICIDES): PARATHION

Availability	6/10
Effectiveness	8/10
Detectability	6/10

This is an agricultural insecticide, widely used in Europe and America. A brown or yellowish liquid, it is usually employed in solution for spraying vegetables and fruit. Its vapour is a toxic nerve gas, capable of killing if inhaled or on contact with the skin.

EFFECTS
- Parathion destroys an enzyme, cholinesterase, which allows the nerves and muscles to function. Symptoms of poisoning, which come on in 30 to 60 minutes, include contraction of the pupils in the eye, headache, abdominal pain, muscle weakness and twitching of the muscles and convulsions. Death results from respiratory failure.
- The lethal dose is 300mg to 400mg.
- As an antidote, antropine (see also BELLADONNA, page 38 and HYOSCINE, page 42) is given in heavy dosage, often exceeding the dangerous level for atropine itself.
- An indication of the presence of parathion in the body would be a very low level of the enzyme cholinesterase.
- Chlorthion and malathion are related to parathion and are equally dangerous pesticides. Chlorthion has in the past been confused with nose drops with fatal results.
- Sarin, another relative of parathion, is also a toxic nerve gas, and only a small drop on the skin is enough to kill a man in fifteen minutes.

REAL-LIFE EXAMPLES
- Many fatalities have occurred with farm workers spraying solutions of parathion against the wind, or collecting fruit which has been previously sprayed, or cleaning aircraft which have been used for spraying.
- Factory workers have also died through absorbing the poison through the skin.
- There have also been a number of reports of murders using parathion from Germany, France and Belgium.

2 POISONS (STREET DRUGS): AMPHETAMINES

Availability	5/10
Effectiveness	6/10
Detectability	8/10

Amphetamine is a powder, but it can also come in liquid form. It usually appears in pills or capsules. It is hardly ever prescribed by doctors nowadays, because of its adverse side effects and habit-forming properties, but it is easy enough to obtain if you know where to go. Street drugs are always cut with fillers, such as sugar, chalk, bicarbonate of soda, etc., so that the amount ingested may be lower than you think.

Amphetamines were once used to suppress appetite and to treat Parkinson's disease, depression, premenstrual tension and hyperactivity in children, but they are no longer used for any of these. They will keep people awake and 'pep pills' or Benzedrine, used to be taken by car or lorry drivers on long journeys. A derivative of amphetamine is called 'speed' and can be injected intravenously. Ecstasy, a derivative of methylenedioxy amphetamine, is now one of the youth scene's favourite drugs, partly because a tablet which costs only between £10 and £25 keeps you going all night. Amphetamines are very addictive and users frequently become anorexic.

EFFECTS
- Amphetamines stimulate muscle and gland cells. Toxic doses taken by mouth will take effect in half an hour to an hour giving rise to insomnia, restlessness, tremors, delirium, sometimes hallucinations and euphoria, and short temper.
- Overdoses can cause cyanosis, convulsions and cerebral haemorrhages leading to strokes and death.
- Administration of amphetamines is especially dangerous to a person who suffers from high blood pressure.
- Amphetamine is not one of the most poisonous substances and a lethal dose would be 3g to 4g of the pure compound.

REAL-LIFE EXAMPLES
- In 1979, Captain Jeffrey MacDonald was convicted of the apparently motiveless murder of his wife and their two baby daughters in North Carolina. Joe McGinnis, in his book on the controversial case *Fatal Vision*, postulates that MacDonald had been taking a slimming preparation containing amphetamines to lose weight and had been working long hours without a break. A night-time domestic quarrel about one of the children wetting the bed, he suggests, escalated into violence. Having killed his wife and eldest child MacDonald then callously killed his youngest and injured himself to make it look like an attack by a gang of hippies. *See* also POLYGRAPH page 101, for more on this case.

2 POISONS (STREET DRUGS): COCAINE

Availability	6/10
Effectiveness	8/10
Detectability	7/10

Cocaine is an alkaloid of the coca plant (*Erythroxylon coca*) which grows in South America. For centuries the natives have chewed the leaves in order to produce exhilarated states in themselves. It also has been used for a number of years in the Western World as a local anaesthetic, but it is little used today because it is so strongly addictive. Sometimes employed in nasal surgery, its ability to constrict blood vessels prevents excessive bleeding. It has nearly always been a drug of abuse and remains so today. In fact, in the United States, it is considered to be the drug which produces the largest illegal income. The pure white cocaine powder is often mixed with baking powder to produce 'rock cocaine' or 'crack' and in this condition it can be smoked. Smoking through a liquid or mixing the drug with ether is sometimes called 'freebasing' and because ether ignites at a very low temperature users have often set themselves alight.

EFFECTS
- Cocaine is absorbed through mucous membranes, particularly in the nose – thus its name 'nose candy' – and also skin cuts. The powder can be inhaled, taken by mouth (this being one of the least effective methods of absorbing the drug) or injected. Like many other alkaloids it affects the central nervous system.
- The symptoms of acute poisoning are hyperactivity, dilated pupils, hallucinations, abdominal pain, convulsions, coma and heart failure.
- Symptoms come on quickly after taking a lethal dose, which can be several grams, and death can take place in a few minutes or up to three hours.

REAL-LIFE EXAMPLES
- There have been many examples of accidental overdoses by cocaine users. Smugglers have also ingested rubber or plastic containers of the drug to get them through customs (they are known as 'swallowers' or 'stuffers') and where these have punctured inside the smuggler's body, fatalities have occurred. It is known as the 'White Death'.

FICTIONAL EXAMPLES
- In the novel *The Glory Game* by Janet Dailey a character dies in an explosion caused by freebasing.

2 POISONS (STREET DRUGS) : HEROIN

Availability	7/10
Effectiveness	8/10
Detectability	7/10

An alkaloid very similar to MORPHINE (*see* page 55), heroin can be made by treating morphine with acetic acid (ethanoic acid). It was originally used medically as a substitute for morphine as its painkilling effects are greater; but it is four times as addictive. In Britain it is still prescribed under the name diacetyl morphine or sometimes just diamorphine, but it is banned for medical use in the United States. As a street drug it goes under the name of 'H', horse, smack, snow, gear, etc. Most of the production of the drug seems to come from the Middle East. It is usually processed in Turkey, and from there smuggled into Europe and America.

EFFECTS
- Like COCAINE (*see* page 62), heroin can be sniffed or smoked by dipping the end of a cigarette in the powder and lighting it. Heroin is sometimes mixed with BARBITURATES (see page 57) and smoked (called 'chasing the dragon') or a solution can be injected under the skin or directly into a vein (intravenously). This last is the quickest way of absorbing the drug and is called 'mainlining'.
- Heroin is something like ten times as poisonous as cocaine, a lethal dose being about 300mg to 400mg. With intravenous injection its effects come on almost immediately and death can take place within minutes. Depression of the nervous system occurs giving rise to pinpoint pupils, shallow respiration, restlessness, cramps, cyanosis, coma and death due to respiratory failure.
- Heroin affects the respiratory system more than morphine, making it more toxic. It leaves no discernible signs in the autopsy, but a blood analysis will reveal the presence of the drug.

REAL-LIFE EXAMPLES
- Actor John Belushi died of a heroin overdose as did singer Janis Joplin and former Los Angeles coroner Thomas Noguchi has stated that many accidental heroin-related deaths are caused by users obtaining and injecting the unexpectedly pure drug.
- Incidentally, the clichéd scene where the detective dips his finger into the white powder to taste for heroin has no basis in fact. It would almost certainly be heavily diluted with a cutting agent, which would mask the bitter taste of heroin, and if it was pure it would be extremely dangerous to taste anyway. You could easily obtain a lethal dose on the end of your finger.

2 SHARP INSTRUMENTS	Availability	9/10
	Effectiveness	7/10
	Detectability	8/10

The most commonly used sharp instrument for murder is the knife. In Britain it is also the most popular method, although in the United States it is only the second most common, behind shooting. The ready availability of kitchen knives makes them a very convenient weapon, though there are available in the shops a wide variety of hunting knives, Scout knives, chef's knives and the handyman-type Stanley knives beloved of young criminals. But other sharp instruments have also been used for murder including bayonets, screwdrivers, scissors, knitting needles, chisels, ice picks and pick axes, pitchforks, carving forks and even electric drills. Serial killer Jeffrey Dahmer killed some of his victims by rendering them unconscious and then boring into their brains with an electric drill.

The ready availability of such implements makes them much more a weapon of sudden anger or impulsive rage than guns or poison, which can indicate a good deal more premeditation.

EFFECTS
● Wounds associated with sharp instruments can be of the cutting or stabbing kind. (See also KNIFE WOUNDS, page 96).
● Stabbing may often leave quite a small hole, with very little exterior bleeding and no indication of the damage done beneath. But if a major blood vessel or an organ like the heart has been damaged, internal bleeding can rapidly cause loss of consciousness and death.

REAL-LIFE EXAMPLES
● Henry Seymour a vacuum cleaner salesman in 1931, stabbed a middle-aged lady in a house in Oxford with a chisel, during a robbery.
● Exiled Russian Revolutionary Leon Trotsky was stabbed to death in Mexico, on the orders of Josef Stalin it was said, in August 1940, by blows to the head with an ice pick.
● In a bizarre case in Warwickshire during February, 1945, farm worker Charles Walton was killed when a pitchfork was plunged into his neck with such force that he was pinned to the ground. His killer was never charged.

FICTIONAL EXAMPLES
● For sheer ingenuity it is hard to beat the weapon devised by Edgar Jepson and Robert Eustace in their story *The Tea Leaf* published in *Strand Magazine*, where a man in a Turkish bath is stabbed with a dagger made of carbon dioxide ice, which vaporises and disappears before the body is discovered.
● *In Billion Dollar Brain* by Len Deighton a female assassin allows her victims to make love to her, then while they are naked and on top of her reaches round and plunges a sharp needle into their spines.

2 STRANGULATION

Availability	8/10
Effectiveness	7/10
Detectability	8/10

Strangulation causes death by ASPHYXIATION (*see* page 11) and can be done with the hands or a ligature. Manual strangulation (throttling) needs a strong person to subdue a weaker one, since the victim will struggle and, if his hands are free, tear at the encircling hands of the attacker. Much more effective is a ligature, which can be a variety of things including a rope or string, a necktie, a scarf or even a belt. The tie can also be knotted in place to keep up the pressure. In cases of homicide the knot on a ligature is always photographed before being removed as it might give clues about the assailant. A very effective ligature is a 'Spanish windlass'. A loop of material is placed around the victim's neck and tightened with a stick, like a tourniquet. If it is done quickly enough, surprising the victim, it could be used by a relatively weak person, since unconsciousness takes place fairly rapidly. The ligature method has been used by many suicides and has even caused accidental death. The American dancer Isadora Duncan was strangled in 1927 when her scarf caught in the wheel of her car.

EFFECTS
- Some of the effects of asphyxiation have already been described.
- Another important effect of strangulation, especially the manual sort, is the damage caused to the thyroid cartilage (the 'Adam's Apple'), the cricoid cartilage and most important of all, the hyoid bone, just above the Adam's Apple. The breaking of this small bone is an almost invariable sign of manual strangulation and can often be seen even if there are no other visible signs.
- Pathologists often X-ray the neck in cases of suspected strangulation before an autopsy takes place so that a fractured hyoid can be observed and the suggestion refuted, as sometimes occurs in court, that it was broken during the post-mortem.

REAL-LIFE EXAMPLES
- Strangulation is a very common method of murder, some ten per cent of all recorded homicides in this country being by strangulation. One of the most famous cases was that of Harold Loughans who had a deformed right hand and was acquitted of murdering a pub landlady in Portsmouth in 1944, because Sir Bernard Spilsbury, the eminent pathologist, said his hand was incapable of exerting enough pressure. Loughans later confessed to the crime.

FICTIONAL EXAMPLES
- In C. S. Forrester's *The Turn Of The Tide*, the killer uses a knotted cord as a garrotte in emulation of the 'Thugs of India'.
- The murderer in *Strangle Hold* by Jerome Doolittle fakes a hospital strangulation, with a flex attached to an emergency button, to make it look like an accident during an auto-erotic episode.

2 SUFFOCATION

Availability	7/10
Effectiveness	6/10
Detectability	8/10

This includes smothering, which works for babies, children or old people who can be held down while a pillow or cushion is pressed over their faces. Sometimes this can be done with unconscious victims or those who are deeply asleep. There have also been cases of accidental suffocation where a drunken person has fallen asleep with their face pressed into a pillow or other enveloping material. Children and some suicides have been suffocated by putting plastic bags over their heads, though these days most manufacturers put holes in this sort of bag to avoid accidents. Criminals who leave victims tied up and gagged, even if the gag leaves the nostrils free, can cause death by suffocation due to a build-up of saliva which blocks air passages. In some instances of this kind a court may reduce a murder charge to MANSLAUGHTER (*see* page 130).

If the oxygen in the atmosphere a person is breathing falls to a low concentration and is replaced with carbon dioxide, death can occur due to a combination of ASPHYXIA (*see* page 11) and carbon dioxide poisoning. This can happen if a victim is trapped in a confined space, and has resulted in the accidental suffocation of people in mineshafts, lifts, cupboards and chests. Children have also died after failing to get out of abandoned refrigerators etc., in which they have been playing. The time it takes to die depends a great deal on the size of the confined space and the rate of metabolism of the victim.

EFFECTS
- These are similar to asphyxiation, though smothering babies with a soft pillow apparently leaves very few signs and in the past these have often been ascribed to cot deaths.

REAL-LIFE EXAMPLES
- Marybeth Tinning, who lived in Schenectady, New York, confessed in 1987 to killing three of her babies by putting a pillow over their faces. The deaths had all been previously put down to misadventure of various kinds.
- In June, 1948, 96-year-old Mrs Lee was found in a trunk in the hall of her seventeen-roomed mansion in Maidenhead. Her arms were tied behind her back and she had been beaten about the head. But she died from suffocation in the trunk, taking, it was estimated, some three to four hours. The lid of a box under her bed yielded two fragmentary fingerprints which led the police to George Russell, a well-known housebreaker. He was convicted of murder and hanged at Oxford in December, 1948.

2 THROAT-CUTTING

Availability	8/10
Effectiveness	6/10
Detectability	9/10

See also KNIFE WOUNDS (page 96). Throat cutting as a form of homicide needs some skill to perform. The best method is to stand behind the victim, force the head back, exposing the throat, and cut across it. For a right-handed person this will produce a slash from left to right – the victim's left to their right – and the direction can be determined by a good pathologist. On the other hand, if the cut is made standing in front of the victim, a right handed assailant will produce a cut from the victim's right to their left. For a successful attack the murderer needs the victim to be either asleep, immobilised or very unprepared, as it is not easy to cut someone's throat if they struggle. In addition, the victim will acquire defensive wounds on the hands or arms as they struggle to ward off the knife or razor. For this reason throat-cutting murders are not that common, although suicide by the same method is relatively well known. The suicide, however, can usually be distinguished by having small trial cuts on his neck, before the fatal incision is made.

EFFECTS
- If cutting the throat severs the main blood vessels, the carotid artery and the jugular vein, death will occur from blood loss, which may be substantial. Cutting the carotid artery can cause blood to spurt several feet. Blood can also block the air passages and death can result from ASPHYXIA (*see* page 11)
- But if a large vein is severed air can be sucked into the blood stream and death can result from EMBOLISM (AIR) (*see* page 23).

REAL-LIFE EXAMPLES
- The most well-known murderer to use throat-cutting was Jack the Ripper.
- Another was Sweeney Todd, the demon barber of Fleet Street, who lived in London in the late 18th century. He is thought to have despatched at least seven clients in this way.
- Serial killers, Peter Kurten (Dusseldorf, 1929-30), Henrich Pommerencke (Black Forest 1959-1960) and Edmund Kemper (California 1972-73) all used throat-cutting.
- Showing that this is by no means a male preserve, Mary Pearcy (London 1890), murdered her lover's wife by cutting her throat.

FICTIONAL EXAMPLES
- *In Murder For Christmas* by Agatha Christie, Mr Lee had his jugular vein severed.

CHAPTER 3

METHODS OF DETECTION AND FORENSIC SCIENCE – INTRODUCTION

In the same way as Chapter 2 the methods in this chapter are given in alphabetical order. The cross-referencing is also the same since it applies throughout the book – entry headings appear in upper case letters whenever they are cross-referenced in the text.

This chapter also includes aspects of forensic science which can help to track down the perpetrator of the crime. There is obviously some overlap with Chapter 4 and the selection of which chapter to put the subject in may seem a little arbitrary. I have selected entries for this chapter on the basis of whether they easily fit in with the summary box system. Marks are given for how easy it is for the detective to observe the phenomenon (a high mark indicates it is relatively easy to observe) and for how useful it is to the investigation. Again, a high mark means a topic is more useful than one with a lower.

The word 'forensic' means the use of various disciplines for the purposes of courts of law. The application of medical studies used to be called Medical Jurisprudence and has always included such topics as pathology and toxicology. The growth of specialisation however has meant that there are today many more disciplines which investigative agencies can make use of. FORENSIC Dentistry or ODONTOLOGY (*see* page 86) is one; *see* also BITE MARK ANALYSIS page 71. Another is Forensic Archaeology, where specialists use their skills to help the police find buried murder victims, using aerial and land surveys involving ground penetration radar. They also advise on the proper way to disinter buried bodies to preserve evidence. Forensic Anthropology is another new specialisation. Here experts study bones, which have usually been buried for some time, to try to identify the victims and to obtain evidence about how they died. FORENSIC PSYCHIATRY and FORENSIC PSYCHOLOGY (*see* pages 87 and 88) are covered elsewhere in this book.

Forensic Science includes FINGERPRINTS (*see* page 84), FIREARMS (*see* pages 25, 26, 27) and BALLISTICS (*see* page 70), the study of FIBRES (*see* page 83), and HAIR (*see* page 91) etc.

As in Chapter 2, for each entry there is an introductory passage and this is usually followed by an Application section which shows how the subject may be applied to the detection process. Real-life examples are given and where appropriate, fictional examples, and the same considerations apply to these sections as in Chapter 2 (see CHAPTER 2 METHODS OF MURDER – INTRODUCTION, page 3).

3 ADIPOCERE

Observability 2/10
Usefulness 8/10

A rare condition, but when it does occur it can be very useful for the investigator. Adipocere is a state a body can reach if left in damp conditions such as in water or in waterlogged soil. The semi-liquid body-fats break down in a process known as saponification and harden to form a white to yellowish-white waxy substance called adipocere. This adheres to the bones helping to preserve the shape of the body and, to some extent, preserving the organs inside. The process, however, takes a long time: four to five months for the face and neck and five to six months for the trunk. But, having been established, adipocere can last for many years, provided the conditions do not change substantially.

APPLICATION

The development of adipocere gives a rough indication of the time of death. But more important, the preservation of the internal organs can give useful information about the death, for example by preserving the contents of the stomach or any injuries the internal organs might have sustained.

REAL-LIFE EXAMPLES

● In June, 1913, two young bodies were found in the Hopetown quarry, near Winchburgh, Scotland. They turned out to be two young boys, one six to seven years old and the other three to four. Both bodies had substantial amounts of adipocere and Professor Harvey Littlejohn from Edinburgh University's Department of Forensic Medicine and his assistant Sidney Smith estimated that the bodies had been in the water about two years. They were even able to examine the contents of the boys' stomachs and decide that they had Scotch broth about an hour before they died. This strongly indicated that the children were local. Eventually, they were identified and their father, Patrick Higgins, convicted of their murder and hanged.

3 BALLISTICS

Observability 8/10
Usefulness 9/10

The science of ballistics is essentially the matching of fired ammunition to the gun which fired it.

APPLICATION

In the case of FIREARMS (RIFLED) (*see* pages 26 and 27) the barrels have spiral grooves cut on the inside. This ensures that the bullet spins when it leaves the barrel, thus improving its accuracy. It also leaves characteristic marks on the bullet. No two barrels will leave quite the same striations. A 'control' bullet is fired from the same barrel and compared with a suspect bullet using a comparison microscope. The suspect bullet may be obtained from a body or the scene of the crime. If it has the same pattern of marks as the control bullet it may be taken that it was fired from the same weapon. The cartridge case will also have marks on it caused by the face of the breech and the striking pin and these also will be able to be compared with a suspect cartridge, if one can be found. These two comparisons give a 'fingerprint' for a particular firearm.

A comparison microscope (*see* also HAIR, page 91 and FIBRES, page 83) has two light tubes, one to view each object to be compared. By means of two mirrors and two prisms the images can be brought together for comparison in the eyepiece.

REAL-LIFE EXAMPLE

● In London, in January 1933, a Cypriot householder was shot dead in his house by a young man who came to the door. Later a young Cypriot pastry cook was arrested and tried for the murder. A .32 Browning pistol, with ammunition already in it, was found in the cellar of the house where the young man lodged. The ammunition was of the same type as the bullet extracted from the body and also one dug out of the wainscot of the murder room. Things looked black for the young pastry cook. Two gun experts hired by the defence, however, were able to show that bullets fired from the gun found in the cellar (and they fired over 50 bullets and examined them) all had the same characteristic marks. And the bullets taken from the body and the wainscoting had none of these. The pastry cook was acquitted.

| **3 BITE-MARK ANALYSIS** | Observability | 8/10 |
| | Usefulness | 7/10 |

Bite-mark analysis forms part of FORENSIC ODONTOLOGY (*see* page 86). Bites may be made on victims of a sexual attack and sometimes even on children, or a bite may be sustained by the perpetrator of an assault, as the victim fights back. Bite-marks may also be found on food, such as apples, chocolate etc.

APPLICATION
In every case the purpose of the analysis is to discover the identity of the biter.

If the bite is comparatively recent, less than five hours old, and made on a human, the skin around the bite may be swabbed and tested. About 80 per cent of the population are 'secretors', that is, their saliva contains the same antigens as their blood and this test will give the perpetrator's blood type. Even better, DNA analysis (*see* page 80) may also be done on the saliva extract.

The bite may then be photographed, drawings made of it and sometimes even cast impressions if the indentations are sufficiently deep. The pattern of teeth marks in a human bite is usually elliptical, but it will vary with the state of the biter's teeth. Any imperfections on the biting surfaces, such as small pits or broken edges, may also show up on the bruise. Bites made during a sexual assault are often accompanied by a sucking action, which causes a reddening over part of the area of the bite. Animal bites, in contrast, usually leave a V-shaped bruise and the teeth frequently puncture and tear the skin.

The next process is to compare the bite mark with the teeth of the suspect. This is done by taking impressions of the teeth and sometimes, if it is necessary to go into court, by making models of the teeth which can be shown to a jury. The scanning electron microscope can be used to magnify minute surface irregularities of the suspect's teeth, for comparison with the bite-mark, as can the electronic image enhancer.

REAL-LIFE EXAMPLES
● Fifteen-year-old Linda Peacock was found strangled to death in a cemetery near Biggar, between Glasgow and Edinburgh, in August, 1967. On one of her breasts was an oval bruise which the pathologist thought was a bite mark. Dr Warren Harvey, Scotland's leading forensic odontologist, was called in and he took dental impressions of 29 youths, all inmates of a nearby youth detention centre. The teeth of one of them, a seventeen-year-old Gordon Hay, fitted the bite-mark and he was subsequently convicted of the murder. It was the first time such evidence had been presented in a Scottish court.

3 BLOOD (BLOODSTAINS)

Observability 9/10
Usefulness 8/10

In a violent homicide there may be a great deal of blood. The human body can contain seven or eight pints (4 to 4.5 litres) and a pint of blood can go a long way – think of spilling a carton of milk. Much can be learned about the assault and the attacker from the bloodstains themselves.

APPLICATION

Drops of blood dripping on to a flat surface will give circular stains with crenated or scalloped edges, and the higher the place from which the blood fell the greater will be the crenation. If the blood hits the surface at an angle (blood dripping on to an inclined surface, for example) the spots will have the shape of an exclamation mark and the greater the angle, the more the stain is elongated. A similarly shaped mark is made when blood is splashed. The small spot at the bottom of the exclamation mark indicates the direction of travel of the blood since it is always in front of the larger blob. Blood can also spurt, if a blow ruptures an artery and this can also give the exclamation-mark stain.

By careful examination of all the blood spots in a confined space, like a room (and they may be on the floor, walls and even the ceiling), the position in which the attacker stood can often be determined. It may also be possible to tell, occasionally, if the assailant was right- or left-handed. A line of blood-spots on the ceiling will often indicate that the attacker has swung a weapon over his head, preparing for another blow.

Large pools of blood show where a bleeding body has been. Blood smears can be caused by the victim crawling about, by being dragged from one position to another, or where the bloodstained murderer has brushed against surfaces.

REAL-LIFE EXAMPLES

● Graham Backhouse called the police one night in April, 1984, to his Cotswold farmhouse. He told them that a neighbour had called and attacked him with a Stanley knife. Backhouse said that he had fled, picked up a shotgun and blasted his attacker, killing the man. Backhouse had fearsome knife wounds on his chest and face, but the blood-splashes in the kitchen, where he said the attack took place, did not fit in with his story. Many of them were round and could only have been made if Backhouse had slashed himself deliberately and stood dripping blood on to the floor to give the appearance of an attack. He was convicted of murder.

3 BLOOD (SEROLOGY)

Observability 7/10
Usefulness 8/10

Serology is the science concerned with serum, roughly speaking the plasma or liquid part of the blood, not the red blood corpuscles; but these days, in forensic work, serology has come to mean any studies with regard to the chemical testing of blood.

APPLICATION

Blood spilt at the scene of a crime, bloodstains on clothing and even dried blood under the finger nails of the victim, can all give information about the victim and sometimes the assailant. But first it must be established that the stain is indeed blood. One test which can be done at the scene of the crime is the peroxidase test. This is merely a screening procedure, however, for other substances can give a positive reaction. Another very sensitive test is the luminol spray, which shows up bloodstains so small that they are invisible to the naked eye, by making them fluoresce.

The next procedure is to check that the material is human and not animal blood and this can be established using the precipitin test. This is done in a laboratory and has given positive results on human blood which has been dried for as long as fifteen years.

Blood-group analysis is also useful and although it cannot give the precise information about identity which can be obtained from DNA PROFILING (*see* page 80), it can be useful for eliminating potential suspects. The simplest system is the ABO system, which is a function of the red blood cells. The blood is classified on the basis of whether it has an agglutinogen in it. Group A contains A agglutinogen and group B contains B agglutinogen. Group AB contains both and group O contains neither. 46 per cent of the white population in this country has group O blood. 42 per cent has group A, 9 per cent group B and only 3 per cent group AB. Blood can sometimes be identified as being male or female by the presence of certain microscopic structures in the white blood cells, or the epithelial cells lining the mouth. If the structures, called Barr bodies, are seen, the blood is usually from a female; they very rarely occur in males.

REAL-LIFE EXAMPLES

● When Lina Lindorfer disappeared from her brother Friedrich's house, where she occupied two rooms, in Bavaria in 1962, most local people thought he had murdered her. But no-one could find the body and, when the local police finally investigated, Friedrich had had plenty of time to scrub the walls, ceilings and floors of the rooms. He even repainted the staircase. The police found nothing. But when the Bavarian State Police were called in and used a luminol spray, they found faint traces of blood all over one of the rooms and the attic. They even built a wooden model of the attic and pin-pointed where all the bloodstains were. When Freidrich Lindorfer saw the model he confessed.

3 BRUISES

Observability 6/10
Usefulness 7/10

Bruises usually occur in response to some injury. Small blood vessels beneath the skin are broken and bleeding occurs into the injured area. If the skin itself is not broken a pool of blood is formed subcutaneously which is then gradually decomposed and absorbed. The red pigment haemoglobin first turns blue as it loses its oxygen, then it is further broken down to green and yellow pigments. The bruise thus changes colour, a process which may take several days or several weeks, depending on where the bruise is and the age of the injured person. A small amount of bruising may not be easily seen on the surface of a dead body, but will be more visible during a post-mortem. Strictly speaking, bruises should not occur after death, since many of the bodily processes then stop. But a heavy blow after death can cause blood vessels beneath the skin to rupture and bleeding can occur. This can usually be distinguished by microscopic examination. Blood in a bruise formed in living tissue will have large numbers of white cells, which the body's immune system will have sent there to combat infection and begin the healing process. Blood from a bruise formed after death will not have such a large proportion of leucocytes.

APPLICATION

The changing colour of a bruise does give some indication of its age, but it is not a reliable indicator. A body with bruises of different colour, however, may give an indication of a series of assaults at different times. This is particularly useful in pin-pointing the physical abuse of children.
The bruising occurring in STRANGULATION (*see* page 65), can often show the marks of fingers and sometimes, if only one hand was used, which one.

REAL-LIFE EXAMPLES

● Reginald Hinks lived in Bath, in 1951, with his elderly father-in-law. One evening, when his wife was out, he rendered the old man unconscious with a blow to the back of the head then put his head in the gas oven. In those days household gas contained CARBON MONOXIDE (*see* page 47) and the old man subsequently died. But he had a bruise at the back of his head. This, Hinks explained, must have happened when he found him and pulled the old man out of the oven. But a pathologist was able to show that the bruise had been caused before death. Hinks was convicted of murder and hanged.

3 CADAVERIC SPASM

Observability 5/10
Usefulness 8/10

This is the 'death grasp', where the dead person at the moment of expiring clasps something in his hand. It is sometimes called 'instantaneous rigor', though it is not thought to have anything to do with RIGOR MORTIS (*see* page 105), the normal stiffening of the body after death. Cadaveric spasm is usually associated with violent death, but in fact it is comparatively rare, which is why the Observability rating is low. When it does occur, however, it is very useful indeed to the crime investigator. Unfortunately, for many would-be murderers and for some crime writers, it cannot be simulated after death. Merely wrapping a dead person's fingers round an object will not give anything like the tightness of grip which a cadaveric spasm produces. And it will be quite obvious to a trained investigator that an attempt has been made to fool the police.

APPLICATION
Hair, fragments of cloth, buttons etc., clutched in a dead person's hand after a violent death can give valuable clues as to what happened at the time of the fatality. One of the 'Brides in the Bath' murderer George Smith's 'wives' was found with a bar of soap clutched in her hand, an indication that her death was both violent and, to her, unexpected. Vegetation caught in the hands of drowning victims can also give valuable information about where the drowning took place.

REAL-LIFE EXAMPLES
- Detective Chief Superintendent William Muncie, in his book *The Crime Pond*, quotes the case of a man found in a clearing in a wood near Murdostoun, Scotland, in October, 1961. Clutched in the man's hand was a collection of pine twigs and other vegetation which made it obvious that the man had been murdered where he lay. He was identified as an inmate of a local mental home and another inmate was eventually convicted of his murder.
- Graham Backhouse, who appeared as an example in BLOOD (BLOODSTAINS) (*see* page 72), tried to bolster his claim that a neighbour had attacked him with a Stanley knife, by placing the knife in the dead man's hand. But the pathologist spotted immediately that it wasn't clutched in a cadaveric spasm.

3 COMPUTERS

Observability 8/10
Usefulness 9/10

The one case which illustrated the need for all major police investigations to have a computer facility was that of the Yorkshire Ripper. Peter Sutcliffe was in fact interviewed nine times, but his name disappeared into the mass of paperwork associated with the case and he never surfaced as the main suspect. It was only when he was picked up in Sheffield in 1981 with a prostitute, and a hammer and a knife were subsequently found nearby, that he really aroused suspicion. Interviewed by the Ripper Squad, he soon confessed.

APPLICATION

In 1987, the Home Office announced the installation of H.O.L.M.E.S. (Home Office Large Major Enquiry System) which was designed to make use of the Police National Computer. Its intention was to allow investigators to enter statements and interviews and build up an index which would allow instant access to names of suspects and other useful information.

The second generation Home Office Computer, called PNCII, was set up at the Metropolitan Police training centre at Hendon in December 1991 and linked by landline with every police force in the country. A policeman anywhere can now access it and be put in possession of vital information. A police patrol following a suspect car, for example, can radio the registration number and within seconds receive the name and address of the registered owner and whether it has been reported stolen. Some forces can also do this using a small computer terminal in the police car which can communicate with the Home Office computer via a satellite. The police patrol can also feed in a name and obtain all the person's previous convictions, whether he is on the run, known to be violent or a drug abuser. Details of stolen property is also held on the computer, including cars, boats and expensive and valuable jewellery.

REAL-LIFE EXAMPLES

● Even before the installation of H.O.L.M.E.S., the police forces of Scotland Yard and the British Transport Police collaborated with the forces of Hertfordshire and Surrey to set up, in July 1985, computer-based Operation Hart to hunt for a criminal known as the Railway Rapist. He was later identified, after he had committed three murders and, with the help of psychological profiling, (*see* FORENSIC PSYCHOLOGY page 88) John Duffy was convicted and given seven life sentences.

3 CONTACT TRACES

Observability 9/10
Usefulness 9/10

One of the basic principles of forensic science, stated by Edmund Locard, Professor of Pathology and Forensic Medicine at the University of Lyon, in 1910, is that every contact leaves a trace. The criminal will always leave something behind at the scene of the crime and take something away. It is up to the crime investigator to discover those traces and link them with the criminal.

This has become so important these days that police forces have scenes of crime officers (SOCOS) and specified procedures for the investigation of the scene of important crimes – see POLICE PROCEDURE (page 135). And many police forces prefer scientific evidence to other kinds, for example, witness identification evidence. It should always be remembered, however, that scientific evidence is only as good as the scientists who produce it, that is, the interpretation they put on the results of the tests, the methods they use and the equipment they employ – these days quite often instrumental equipment. The well-known miscarriage of justice concerning the Maguire family (1976) and the Birmingham Six Case (1975) occurred in part due to the use of a test for nitroglycerine which was not specific enough for the required determination.

APPLICATION
Contact traces fall into a number of sections:

1. FINGERPRINTS (*see* page 84), hand or palm prints, footprints and marks left by shoes, vehicle tyres, etc. The recognisable imprint of a victim's face once appeared on the windscreen of a car which hit her.

2. Marks left by tools, such as jemmies, on wood or other surfaces at the scene of the crime. The blade of a particular tool will carry minute imperfections which can often be seen by microscopic examination and can help to identify it.

3. FIBRES (*see* page 83) and other material from the clothes of the criminal, or substances, for example, sand, which have come from the clothing and can help to establish his job, mode of living or where he comes from. This type of material is often vacuumed up or scraped from under the victim's fingernails.

4. Stains such as BLOOD (*see* page 72), semen, sweat, saliva or urine.

5. Biological substances, such as HAIR (*see* page 91), and plant material, such as seeds, leaves and soil.

6. Trace materials carried away by the criminal, such as paint or other stains on his clothes, his vehicle or tools used in the crime. Chemicals on his hands, if he has handled explosives or fired guns.

3 CRIME KITS   Observability 7/10
                                     Usefulness   9/10

The old 'murder bag', which Chief Inspectors of Scotland Yard's Murder Squad used to carry when they left London to take charge of some murder investigation for another force, was invented in the 1920s. Sir Bernard Spilsbury, the famous pathologist, was so appalled to see Scotland Yard men handling pieces of a body with their bare hands, that he, in collaboration with senior officers, put together a collection of things which an investigating officer would need. They included rubber gloves, paper bags and other receptacles for the collection of small pieces of evidence, tape measures, a compass, apparatus to take fingerprints and a magnifying glass. Nowadays, such is the sophistication of modern murder investigations, especially among the larger forces, that the man in charge, although he will wear rubber gloves, will hardly touch anything at the murder scene. Scenes of crime officers (SOCOS) will collect evidence. Fingerprint teams will examine the scene and photographic teams do the appropriate recording. The police surgeon will pronounce the victim dead and also make his initial examination.

All these experts will have their kits. SOCOS' evidence-collection kit will have paper bags for anything that is likely to be damp, since it can dry out in paper, whereas in a plastic bag it would rot. Plastic bags and bottles are used for anything where the liquid must be preserved and for FIBRES (*see* page 83), which must not be placed in paper since paper itself has fibres. Large cardboard boxes are useful for larger items. All items are individually bagged, bottled or packaged and labelled as to source, time of collection, etc.

Specially prepackaged kits are available commercially for collecting and preserving gunpowder residues, blood samples and for rape analysis samples.

FINGERPRINT (*see* page 84) kits have been in use for a very long time and are now available to cope with practically every conceivable requirement.

Photographic kits today contain a wide range of cameras, both still and video, and ancillary equipment.

The police surgeon, in addition to carrying the usual doctor's bag, will also have equipment allowing him or her to make diagrams of wound sites, and will have available microscope slides and containers for collecting specimens. Plastic bags are also used to cover the victim's hands, to preserve clutched material, and also to cover and preserve the head.

3 DECOMPOSITION (PUTREFACTION)   Observability   6/10
                                        Usefulness   7/10

The decomposition of the human body begins sometime after death. Useful evidence may be obtained, mainly about the time of death, by the state of putrefaction which the body has reached.

APPLICATION
Decomposition, ignoring insect infestation (FORENSIC ENTO-MOLOGY *see* page 85), begins properly when RIGOR MORTIS (*see* page 105) departs, after about 48 hours for a body left in the air and up to four days for one immersed in water. Putrefaction is caused by bacteria which normally live in the intestines, and, after death, spread through the body by way of the blood vessels. A greenish colouration appears on the abdomen after two or three days followed by discoloration of the veins which become prominent, causing a 'marbling' effect. The body begins to swell after five to six days as gases accumulate and if the body is immersed in water at this stage it may float to the surface.

Factors which affect the decomposition process are:

Air: Free circulation of moist warm air encourages putrefaction and lack of it slows down the process. Thus a naked body decomposes faster than a clothed one and a buried one slower still.

Temperature: Putrefaction sets in at about 10°C and works best between 21°C and 38°C. Above this temperature, the body may dry out and the process will be slowed down; sometimes, even, preservation may occur by MUMMIFICATION (*see* page 98).

Moisture: The process needs moisture but this is usually supplied from the body's own fluids.

Age and state of body: Young people decay more quickly than old because they have more fat and the bodies of obese people decompose more easily than those of thin.

Some poisons, such as arsenic and antimony, retard the process and preserve the body.

REAL-LIFE EXAMPLES
● Leslie Harvey, redecorating his mother's house in Rhyl, in May 1960, while she was in hospital, opened a cupboard at the top of the stairs which he had never seen open before. Inside was the mummified body of a woman. It was estimated it had been there twenty years and the warm dry flow of air through the cupboard had preserved the body. When what looked like a ligature was found round the neck Mrs Harvey was charged with murder. She admitted putting the body in the cupboard but denied murder. The evidence for strangulation was not strong and she was acquitted. She was convicted of drawing the woman's pension for twenty years.

3 DNA PROFILING

Observability 5/10
Usefulness 9/10

DNA profiling is undoubtedly one of the most important techniques of modern forensic science. Developed by Professor Alec Jeffreys of Leicester University in 1984, it enables the positive identification of individuals from a minute trace of body fluid, a fragment of hair or even bone.

APPLICATION

All animal cells contain DNA (deoxyribonucleic acid). It is an immensely long molecule which contains, among other things, sequences of just four smaller molecules called bases. There are something like three billion of these in an average DNA molecule and no two people will have exactly the same sequence. It is impractical to treat the whole molecule, but it is possible to cut it up into smaller pieces containing only ten to fifteen bases at a time. These fragments can then be separated and visualised using radioactive DNA probes and an X-ray film. Bands appear on the film like a supermarket bar code and this is sometimes called a genetic fingerprint of a DNA profile. Since half a person's DNA is obtained from his mother and half from his father the bands can also be used to establish parentage.

It is in the region of identity, however, that DNA is most useful in criminal cases. Blood or semen left at the scene of the crime can be submitted to DNA analysis and compared with samples from suspects, or bloodstains on clothes of the suspect could be DNA analysed and compared with that of the victim.

But there are drawbacks to DNA profiling. Because only a portion of the DNA molecule is taken it has to be assumed that the bands present in a DNA profile are distributed randomly in a population and the chance of an accidental match (a false positive) occurring can be calculated statistically. But in certain communities people may marry distant relatives and genetic characteristics may not be distributed in a random manner. In addition, DNA testing is a complicated procedure and contamination of the sample, with DNA from other sources, such as fungi or bacteria, must be carefully excluded. DNA itself may degrade, if it becomes too warm or in the presence of moisture, and this can result in too few or too many DNA fragments.

REAL-LIFE EXAMPLES

● When two teenaged schoolgirls were raped and strangled, one in November 1983 and the other in July 1986, near Leicester, the local police decided to test the DNA of all the local men. The results were negative. But then one young man admitted he'd taken the test for a friend, Colin Pitchfork. Pitchfork was tested and his DNA matched that of the semen in the two girls. He was convicted of murder, in 1987, the first in this country using DNA evidence.

● But DNA evidence was rejected by the jury in the case of O.J. Simpson in Los Angeles, when the defence claimed that the samples were contaminated during handling by the L.A. police department.

3 EXHUMATION

Observability 5/10
Usefulness 7/10

Exhumation – digging up a body which has been officially buried – must be authorised in this country by the Home Secretary, usually on the request of the police or a coroner.

APPLICATION
A mechanical digger may be used to remove part of the grave soil, but careful removal is required further down since samples of soil must be taken from above, below and on both sides of the coffin if poisoning is suspected, since some poisons like arsenic can be present in surprisingly large amounts in soil.

The disinterment is supervised by the police. In addition there will be present the undertaker, to identify the coffin, a pathologist and possibly other scientists to collect samples.

The coffin is removed to the mortuary. Sometimes the lid may be lifted slightly in the open air to allow noxious gases to escape, but the coffin is only opened properly at the mortuary. Photographs are taken of the body and the body must be identified either by the undertaker, a relative or by fingerprints or dental records. It is then removed from the coffin. If poisoning is suspected, samples of the coffin wood itself will be taken and anything which has been in contact with the body, such as the shroud and the coffin lining. The body is X-rayed and a full autopsy carried out.

If the body has been embalmed vital evidence will probably have been lost since most of the blood is replaced with embalming fluid. The state of the body depends a great deal on the conditions in the cemetery. Warm damp conditions will lead to rapid decomposition whereas cold dry conditions will help to preserve it.

REAL-LIFE EXAMPLES
● The death rate at the Archer Home for Elderly People in Hartford, Connecticut, in 1914, was six times the regional average. The police were called in and they exhumed five bodies, all of which were adjudged to have died from arsenic poisoning. Amy Archer-Gilligan, the proprietress, was charged with murder. After a retrial she eventually confessed and died in prison.
● Mrs Edith Rosse died in 1934 in London. She had been sharing a house with Maundy Gregory, the so-called 'Great Swindler' who was later involved in the 'titles for sale' scandal, and in whose favour she had just altered her will. Suspicions were later expressed that he had been responsible for her death and her body was exhumed. But Gregory had arranged for it to be buried only eighteen inches deep in an unlined coffin in a graveyard close to a river. In the winter, the cemetery was regularly flooded. When the coffin was disinterred, water poured out of it and, not surprisingly, no poison was discovered in the body. The coroner's jury returned an open verdict.

3 FACIAL RECONSTRUCTION

Observability 4/10
Usefulness   7/10

This is not such a modern technique as one might imagine. Many of the measurements, on which building up a face and head from a skull are based, were made in Switzerland at the turn of the century. The first man really to construct faces on a large scale was a Russian, Mikhail Gerasimov, who began his work in the 1920s. The scientist who brought the technique to prominence in this country was Richard Neave of the Manchester University Department of Medical Illustration. The technique has been used to give faces to historical figures, for example Phillip of Macedonia and Tamerlane The Great, but although not used a great deal in this country it has great potential for identifying homicide victims from their skulls.

APPLICATION

The principle of facial reconstruction is that the face is determined largely by the skull beneath, and by the application of certain rules the face can be reconstructed with a surprising degree of accuracy.

First any flesh is removed from the skull and any broken or missing pieces of the skull repaired or replaced. Then a cast is made of the skull and it is from this that the face is built up. Small holes are drilled into the cast at specific points and small wooden pegs (cocktail sticks are often used) inserted so that they stick out of the plaster a predetermined amount corresponding to the thickness of the flesh at those points. The facial muscles are then built up to the top of the pegs using modelling clay. The nose, ears and facial hair, like eyebrows, are largely a matter of experience, though tufts of hair adhering to the skull can give information about the length of the subject's hair and its type.

A more modern technique uses a laser beam reflected from the skull to establish the contours, which are then compared with the head of a living person of similar appearance which is scanned in the same way. A computer gives the measurement of tissue thicknesses on the unknown skull, which are fed to a milling machine which sculpts the head from hard plastic, final touches being added by an experienced sculptor.

REAL-LIFE EXAMPLES

● In December 1987, a body was discovered by workmen digging a trench in a back garden in Cardiff. It was that of a teenaged girl and little remained except the bones. Richard Neave reconstructed the face from the skull, which was shown on BBC Television's *Crimewatch UK* programme. She was recognised as a young teenaged runaway called Karen Price and the identification confirmed by dental records. Two men were eventually convicted of her murder.

3 FIBRES   Observability   7/10
                                                 Usefulness   6/10

Fibres like HAIRS (*see* page 91) are some of the commonest materials transferred between victim and assailant or left at the scene of the crime. They can be identified with great accuracy by modern forensic techniques, but form only part of the chain of circumstantial evidence. They often do not have the usefulness for personal identification that FINGER-PRINTS (*see* page 84) or DNA PROFILING (*see* page 80) have.

APPLICATION

Fibres can be either natural or man-made. Natural fibres can be further subdivided into Animal, such as wool, silk, mohair, and Vegetable, including cotton, hemp, jute and lint. Man-made fibres are manufactured by liquifying a substrate, which can be natural polymeric material, for example, rubber, proteins or cellulose; synthetics such as nylon and polyester and even substances like glass or metals. The liquid is then squirted through small holes to make long strands and allowed to solidify.

The microscope is used extensively to identify natural fibres and with man-made fibres birefringence, which involves measuring the refractive index of the material, is often useful.

Crime-writers should remember that it may be possible to say that a particular fragment of fibre, found for example under the fingernails of a victim, came from the material from which the suspect's coat was made. But it may not be possible to say that it came from that particular coat, since there may be hundreds like it in the shops.

The value of fibre evidence is usually in the investigation and in building up a case against the accused. The more incriminating examples the better is the case.

REAL-LIFE EXAMPLES
● An example of conclusive fibre evidence came in 1940, when a fifteen-year-old girl was found murdered in a concrete blockhouse near Liverpool. In the litter on the floor Dr J. B. Firth, Director of the North Western Forensic Science Laboratory, found a small piece of fabric which had been part of a military field dressing and it was impregnated with the antiseptic acriflavine. Samuel Morgan, a young soldier, was suspected since he had a cut on his thumb. His sister produced a discarded portion of a similar dressing she had put on her brother's thumb. Dr Frith was able to match the two pieces and show they came from the same dressing. Morgan was convicted of murder.
● In November, 1976, the body of a young Boy Scout was found near the Leeds-Bradford Airport. Nylon fibres on the body could have come from the carpet in a car. A long investigation finally unearthed a carpet fitter who had just such a carpet in his car. But he had since sold the car. The new owner was eventually traced and confessed to having killed the young boy.

3 FINGERPRINTS
Observability 8/10
Usefulness 9/10

Fingerprint identification has been in use for over a hundred years and is still one of the most important tools in crime investigation.

APPLICATION

Fingerprints may be made in a number of ways: impressions in soft materials, such as putty, soap or chocolate and visible marks made on surfaces by a dirty or bloody hand. These are called 'visuals' and can be photographed, or more commonly lifted by a transparent adhesive tape which can then be transferred to a card for photographing and recording. The third category are deposits of natural secretions of the skin. These are usually invisible and are called 'latents'. They can be visualised by dusting them with powder, usually black, but it can be white or even red, or various chemical reagents. Iodine vapour has been used, ninhydrin solution; sometimes even Super Glue can be employed for difficult cases. The object having latents on it must be sealed in a container with Super Glue vapour for several hours. Electrostatic methods and fluorescence techniques are useful and for obtaining prints from human skin an X-ray method has been developed. The only surfaces you cannot obtain fingerprints from are rough wooden surfaces, bricks and stone and most cloth. On a hard smooth surface in cold dry weather prints will be lost quickly, but in warm moist weather they will last weeks or months and a fingerprint was raised on an Egyptian papyrus over 2,000 years old, of the scribe who wrote it.

Fingerprint classification is complicated and various systems are in use. A common one is the Henry system, which is based on four ridge patterns: arches, loops, whorls and compounds (combinations of the others). Identification results from matching fingerprints. In this country there must be sixteen points of resemblance before a match can be claimed, but the number varies in other countries and in the USA there is no standard at all.

REAL-LIFE EXAMPLES

● In March 1977 a mummified body was found in a shopping trolly in Rochdale. No facial features were left and the hands were badly decayed. Detective Chief Inspector Fletcher, in charge of Manchester's fingerprint bureau, who had just obtained the prints from an Egyptian mummy, tried the same technique with the body, using dental putty on the fingertips to obtain a mould. From this the body was identified as James Finley. His wife claimed he had committed suicide and she was convicted only of concealing a death.

● Peter Griffiths was convicted of the murder of a young child in Blackburn hospital in 1948, after his prints were discovered on a large bottle in the children's ward. The whole town of Blackburn had been fingerprinted. Over 46,000 fingerprints were recorded, the largest number, at that time, ever taken for one investigation.

3 FORENSIC ENTOMOLOGY

Observability 7/10
Usefulness 8/10

The gases which a dead body gives off attract flies and a study of the maggots they produce can give information about the time of death, even for bodies which have been buried for years.

APPLICATION

Luckily, flies find the temperature of the living body, 37°C, too high for them. But when the temperature has dropped to below 30°C, usually some six to eight hours after death, depending on the weather conditions, flies will then lay their eggs in it. In this country these will normally be house flies, blue- and green-bottles and blowflies. They lay their eggs in moist shady conditions, like the eyes and the orifices of the body and also open wounds. The eggs will hatch in eight to fourteen hours, but this again depends on the body temperature and the conditions outside the body. The maggots will then start to feed on the dead flesh. They eat mainly protein material but not fat, nails or hair. As they eat they grow and like all creatures with an outer shell they must replace it as they grow. Maggots go through three stages or 'instars'. The first occurs after two or three days, the second seven or eight days and the third ten to twelve days. Each of these stages can be recognised by entomologists. After reaching the third stage the maggots usually fall off the body and go into the pupal stage, where another hard case is made, and from this the adult flies emerge in about twelve days. The empty cases remain for years. Study of the insect debris will give the minimum time since the infestation began. The maximum is more difficult to measure because it depends very much on the conditions which the body has experienced.

For bodies which have been buried in the ground, Phorid flies, sometimes called coffin flies, are useful. They burrow into the soil and feed on dead bodies, stripping off the flesh. When the bones are exposed, fungus begins to grow on them and woodlice graze on the fungus. Experts can tell how long these colonies take to develop and thus how long the body has been buried.

REAL-LIFE EXAMPLES

● On a day in early June, 1964, two boys discovered a body in Bracknell Woods, Berkshire. Pathologist Professor Keith Simpson describes in his book, *Forty Years Of Murder*, how he found blue-bottle maggots on the body. They were of the third stage, but had not yet become pupas. From this he estimated that the body had been there nine or ten days, putting death at 16 or 17 June. The body was identified and a suspect, William Brittle charged with the murder. He produced a witness who said he had seen the murdered man alive on 20 June. But Simpson's evidence held up in court and Brittle was convicted of murder.

3 FORENSIC ODONTOLOGY

Observability 8/10
Usefulness 8/10

This is, in part, the identification of dead bodies by an examination of their teeth, which is an extremely useful aid to the investigation of crime. (*See* also BITE MARK ANALYSIS page 71).

APPLICATION

Teeth, including the root structures, and the materials used to repair and replace them, are some of the most durable substances in the human body. Like bones, they resist the ordinary processes of decay and often survive if the body is burnt or consumed by acids. The murderer John Haig, who admitted to destroying nine bodies with acid, failed to completely get rid of the last one, Mrs Durand-Deacon, and an acrylic plastic denture was identified as belonging to her.

No two sets of teeth are the same. Apart from the initial differences, there will be natural wear, extractions and fillings etc., which will all be different for individual people. And techniques such as X-ray examination have enabled internal structures, for example root and crown formation and clinical eruption of teeth, to be examined. In fact, a person's dental chart has been compared with a fingerprint.

In addition, up to about 25 years the age of a person can be determined from the eruption of their teeth. After this it is more difficult, although techniques based on the wear of the enamel have been successful. Some racial differences have also been observed, by the shape of teeth, and sometimes cultural dictates give useful indications. Many wealthy Orientals for example have a liking for gold capping of teeth, which appears to be purely for decoration. One of the problems of identification by examination of teeth, however, is the sheer scale of the task. There are millions of dental charts filed away in dentists' surgeries and matching a completely unknown set of teeth can be a major problem.

Scotland Yard have set up a central index of dental records for missing persons. When a person is reported missing their dentist is asked to supply a dental chart which can be used as a comparison if an unidentified body is found.

REAL-LIFE EXAMPLE
● When workmen clearing a bombed chapel in South London in July 1942 came across a body it was thought at first to be a bomb victim. But the head had been cut off, several limbs severed and an attempt had been made to burn the body. Plainly this was done to make identification difficult, if not impossible. The lower jaw was missing, but dental charts of the upper identified her as Rachel Dobkin, the estranged wife of the fire-watcher at the chapel, Harry Dobkin. He was tried for her murder, convicted and hanged.

3 FORENSIC PSYCHIATRY

Observability 6/10
Usefulness 8/10

The psychiatrist deals with abnormal mental states and the psychologist with normal; see also FORENSIC PSYCHOLOGY (page 88). Forensic psychiatrists will advise courts, solicitors, and prison and probationary services both on the mental states of individuals and on their treatment, but the most important functions, as far as crime writers are concerned, are the advice they give in the assessment of defences to murder and competence to stand trial.

Unfit to plead

After arrest, a person accused of murder will usually be remanded in custody, and at this stage they may be examined by psychiatrists if the prosecution has doubts about their ability to understand a subsequent trial, or the defence submits that the prisoner is unfit to plead. A special jury then judges the psychiatric evidence and, if it decides that the verdict is 'unfit to plead', the prisoner will be confined to a mental hospital, 'without limit of time', or until judged sane enough to stand trial.

Insanity

This old defence to MURDER (*see* page 133) is embodied in the McNaghten Rules, which say that a 'not guilty through insanity verdict' can be reached if a defendant did not know the nature and quality of his act, or, if he did know this, didn't know it was wrong. This was very difficult to prove and many people we would consider insane today were previously convicted of murder and many were hanged.

Diminished Responsibility

A defence allowed since 1957 and stating that if the defendant was suffering at the time of the crime from such an abnormality of mind that his responsibility was impaired, then he should not be convicted or murder, but convicted on the lesser charge of MANSLAUGHTER (*see* page 130).

AUTOMATISM (*see* page 12).

Another defence to murder which the forensic psychiatrist is asked to advise upon, but it is covered elsewhere in this book.

INFANTICIDE (see page 127)

This defence can be offered by mothers, in the case of the death of babies under a year old, that they had not recovered from the effects of childbirth or the effects of lactation. Again, a successful plea reduces conviction to one of manslaughter.

REAL-LIFE EXAMPLES

● It is interesting that, in a recent case, ten-year-olds Robert Thompson and Jon Venables were found guilty of the murder of two-year-old Jamie Bulger, but 30 years ago eleven-year-old Mary Bell, who killed two children, was convicted only of manslaughter due to diminished responsibility.

3 FORENSIC PSYCHOLOGY (PSYCHOLOGICAL PROFILING)

Observability 5/10
Usefulness 8/10

The observability rating for this is low because it is not that often met with in the investigation of serious crime. Although psychiatrists deal with abnormal mental states and psychologists with normal, the distinction becomes somewhat blurred in the case of psychological profiling, since although the technique was largely invented by an American psychiatrist it is quite often used by psychologists.

APPLICATION

Scotland Yard have always kept files on the operating methods of criminals, but even before this, anthropologists, in particular, Cesare Lombrosco (1876), tried to establish the types of people who would commit crimes. But it was mainly the work of the American psychiatrist James A. Brussel, who studied a criminal's actions to try to find out what sort of person he was, which put many of these ideas on a practical basis. In 1957, he successfully created a profile for the Mad Bomber of New York, who for 16 years had kept up a bombing campaign which terrorised the population. When the man was finally apprehended he turned out to be remarkably like the profile.

In the 1970s the FBI established the Behavioural Science Unit at the National Academy in Quantico and used the disciplines of the behavioural scientist, psychologist and psychiatrist, to try to construct profiles of serial killers in America. In 1985, they introduced the Violent Crime Apprehension Programme (VICAP), a central information system collecting and analysing reports on criminals from all over the USA to try and reveal early patterns of serial killing.

A profile on an unknown killer contains both physical and psychological elements and is compiled from witness reports, the type of victim, method of killing etc.

REAL-LIFE EXAMPLES

● In April 1986 David Canter, Professor of Applied Psychology at the University of Surrey, was asked to help in the hunt for a serial killer. Known as the Railway rapist, the man had raped 30 women, near railway stations in the London and surrounding area, since he began in 1982. And he had killed three women as well. Professor Canter, by studying the reports of the crimes, was able to produce a psychological profile. This contained 17 elements, such as the area he lived in, what he did for a living, his age range and his physical size, the fact that he was married but had no children and that his marriage was in serious trouble. When the man, John Duffy, was finally caught, 13 out of the 17 parameters, including the ones I have mentioned, were shown to be correct.

3 GLOVE PRINTS

Observability   4/10
Usefulness   6/10

It has been known for a long time that fingerprints could be obtained under certain conditions from the inside of some gloves, particularly rubber or plastic gloves, when the hands of the suspect were very dirty or sweaty. And if such an article was left at the scene of the crime it could yield valuable information about who had worn it. And in the 1970s, research at the fingerprint bureau at Scotland Yard showed that prints could even be obtained from the outside of some gloves.

APPLICATION
The material of which a glove is made, leather or plastic or wool, will leave its own characteristic marks on a surface due to the microscopic structure of the material and because the wear of a glove will add its own particular pattern of creases and holes and scars. It was found that rubber kitchen gloves, for example, because of the moulding process by which they are made, produced an individual fingerprint caused by microscopic imperfections on the surface of the material. And the dirt a glove picks up helps to impress this pattern on any surface it touches.

REAL-LIFE EXAMPLES
- In 1971, after a burglar alarm had been set off, a man was apprehended running from a building in South London. Fingerprint experts found a glove print from the scene of the attempted break-in which matched one of the left-hand fingers of the suspect's suede gloves. He was duly convicted in May and this was the first time such evidence had been successful in a British court.
- A thief in Manchester blew open the door of a post-office safe, but left behind a pair of rubber gloves. The safe-blower's hand must have been covered in grease because on the inside of the gloves was a complete set of his fingerprints.

3 GUNSHOT WOUNDS

Observability   8/10
Usefulness   9/10

The appearance of the entrance and exit wound, if any, informs about the calibre of the bullet and the distance from which it was fired.

APPLICATION

Where the weapon is held against the skin (contact wound) the bullet produces a round hole. This is slightly larger than the diameter of the bullet, surrounded by a burn from the flame produced at the muzzle. Soot, which blackens the skin, is also present, but can be washed off. If the contact is above a bone, such as a head wound, or a chest wound above the sternum, a starshaped hole is obtained due to the hot gases being held up by the bone and ballooning the skin.

Intermediate-range entrance wounds will have an abrasion ring round the hole and are characterised by tattooing, caused by the expelled powder grains becoming embedded in the skin. This cannot be washed off. For most handguns, tattooing occurs up to distances of two feet and for rifles up to three feet. Longer range projectiles will leave no powder or soot deposits, but will have an abrasion ring and the diameter of the hole will be slightly less than the calibre of the bullet, due to the elasticity of the skin.

Wounds from bullets entering at an angle will have an oval shape and at close range an oval deposit of soot. Exit wounds are larger than entrance, have a more irregular shape and no abrasion rings.

Shot has little penetrating power, so shotgun injuries do not usually incorporate an exit wound. Up to about two feet away, the shot will not spread and a more or less solid mass of metal shot and wadding will rip into the body, giving tattooing and scorching. Between two and three feet a ragged wound is produced and beyond about four feet the shot begins to spread giving a central wound with perforations around it. A rough guide to distance is to measure in inches the diameter of the wound to the furthest pellet mark and subtract one, which gives the distance from which the shot was fired in yards.

Chemicals produced in the discharge of a weapon will often blow back on to the hands of the person firing it. These can be detected, provided the test is done within a few hours, by swabbing the suspect's hands with dilute nitric acid and testing the washings. More accurate results can be obtained using neutron activation analysis.

REAL-LIFE EXAMPLES

● Mrs Merrett was found in her sitting-room in Edinburgh, in March, 1926, with a bullet in her head. Her son Donald said she had shot herself. Tried for her murder, his defence produced the eminent pathologist Sir Bernard Spilsbury, who said that the lack of tattooing round the wound could be explained by it being washed off by the blood. Surprisingly, this erroneous conclusion was accepted by the jury and Donald walked free.

3 HAIR
Observability 7/10
Usefulness 7/10

We have all seen the headlines: 'Killer convicted by a single hair,' but unfortunately such statements are not true. Evidence solely from hair is simply not enough to establish guilt, unless cells from the root of the hair can be obtained and they remain fresh enough to do DNA PROFILING (see page 80). But having said all that, a great deal of useful information may be obtained from hair.

APPLICATION
Hair can be from the head, eyebrows and eyelashes, facial hair, such as moustaches and beards, underarm hair, pubic hair and hair from the rest of the body. And, in cross-section, under a microscope all these different types can easily be distinguished by an expert.

Unless burnt or treated with harsh chemicals, hair lasts as long as a skeleton. It also retains many chemicals, such as ARSENIC (*see* page 46) and ANTIMONY (*see* page 45) and can indicate the way it was administered – a series of small doses or one large one. Hair has also been examined for street drugs, again to establish the pattern of usage, but doubt has been expressed about these results since it is not impossible for hair to pick up chemicals from the environment. Hair can sometimes be used to establish racial origin, Negroid and Caucasian hair being easily distinguished, for example.

The comparison MICROSCOPE, (*see* also page 70), is useful in establishing the possibility that hairs left at the scene of the crime can be associated with a suspect. Neutron Activation Analysis can determine the different elements in a single human hair and this also helps to establish a link with hair from a suspect and that left at the scene of the crime.

If hair is pulled out, it will often have cells adhering to the root. These can give information about the owner's blood group and, if they are fresh enough, DNA PROFILING (*see* page 80), can also be done.

REAL-LIFE EXAMPLES
● Hair evidence played a vital part in the case of the murder of eight-year-old Helen Priestly, whose body was found in a sack in the corridor of a tenement in Aberdeen in April, 1934. A neighbour, Mrs Jeannie Donald, who was known to be on bad terms with the child was charged with her murder and bloodstains and bacteria found on Helen's clothes matched those found in Donald's flat. In addition, hairs which could have come from the accused were found in the sack. Mrs Donald was convicted of murder.
● John Collins, the Michigan co-ed killer, was trapped in 1969, by tiny hair clippings found in a basement he had access to and which had come from his cousins who had had their hair cut down there. The clippings were found to be very similar to those found in the underclothing of his seventh victim, showing that he must have killed her in the basement before dumping the body elsewhere.

3 HEAD WOUNDS

Observability 8/10
Usefulness 7/10

APPLICATION

The cause of fatal head injuries can be difficult to assess. Was the blow delivered intentionally or accidentally? Some blows, such as those delivered by a hammer or other blunt instrument will drive broken pieces of the skull into the brain, leaving a hole the shape of the weapon and cracks radiating from the point of impact. Information can still be obtained even if the body has largely decomposed. Painstakingly putting together the pieces of a smashed skull has in the past yielded valuable evidence about the cause of death.

Death can also result from a blow which does not shatter the skull, but damages the brain directly beneath the site of impact. This usually happens when the head is still. Another type of brain injury includes damage to the opposite side of the brain in addition to beneath the point of contact. This most often occurs with a moving head and is called a 'contre coup'. It is thought to occur as the brain literally bounces around inside the skull. Boxers sometimes sustain this kind of injury and it can also be caused by a fall. Tumbling over backwards and hitting the back of the head on a hard surface can fracture the skull at the back and damage the frontal lobes as well.

REAL-LIFE EXAMPLES

● William Moore, a prominent Kentucky architect, was having marriage problems. After he and his wife rowed one night in December 1970, they slept in separate rooms in their Louisville home. The next morning Moore found his wife in the bathroom with a severe head injury. He called for medical help, but she died in hospital. The police were notified and he was charged with her murder. At his trial the prosecution contended that he had struck his wife with a blunt instrument. But the defence brought in the eminent New York pathologist Dr Milton Helpern, who having done his own autopsy concluded that the brain injury was a case of 'contre coup', most likely caused by an accidental fall in the bath. But it didn't convince the jury, who brought in a verdict of guilty and Moore was sentenced to 21 years in prison. But in 1974 the state governor reviewed the case and decided that the medical evidence on which Moore had been convicted was in error and he was released.

3 HYPNOSIS

Observability 6/10
Usefulness 5/10

Hypnotism has been known since at least the times of the Greeks and Romans, but it was not until the late 1700s that the Austrian physician Franz Mesmer brought it to prominence in Europe.

APPLICATION

It is said that it is impossible to hypnotise a person against their will, so it appears that fiction stories where a victim is hypnotised and made to commit a crime, which they afterwards forget, do not have a lot of basis in fact, although it is not unknown for criminals to use this as a defence. It seems that active co-operation is required before a person can slip into the trance-like state, where they become very susceptible to suggestion.

Hypnotism has its uses in relaxation techniques and witnesses to a horrible crime can sometimes be calmed down during a trance. The significant thing, as far as many police forces are concerned, is that witnesses may remember things under hypnosis they cannot remember in the waking state. There have undoubtedly been some notable successes in this area, like the Los Angeles Police Department who employed hypnosis on a driver of a hijacked school bus who was too shocked to remember much. Under hypnosis he was able to describe the hijackers and even remember the number of the get-away car. However, some experts have questioned the value of such techniques, pointing out that the increased susceptibility to suggestion and 'leading questions' under hypnosis, makes the accuracy of the information obtained suspect.

REAL-LIFE EXAMPLES

● An eighteen-year-old woman shot and seriously wounded two United States Marshals in 1981 while attempting to help her husband escape from custody. She claimed that he had been hypnotising her for a long time, telling her he was God, and when she fired the gun she believed that God was telling her to do it. The woman was acquitted of the charge of assault with intent to commit murder.
● Kenneth Bianchi, one of the Hillside Stranglers of Los Angeles, who committed their murders between 1977 and 1979, exhibited multiple personality traits under hypnosis. In particular, a character called Steve emerged who spoke with a different voice and admitted to all the atrocities. But sceptics pointed out that Steve bore a remarkable resemblance to a living person, a psychiatry graduate whose name and academic records Bianchi had stolen and used to set himself up as a consultant.

3 IDENTIFICATION (IDENTITY PARADES)   Observability   9/10
Usefulness   4/10

APPLICATION
Witness descriptions of suspected criminals and witness identifications are the cornerstone of police detective work. Programmes like *Crimewatch UK* and *Crimestoppers* are continually asking for the public to recognise faces they may have seen at some location in the past, descriptions of people they might know, cars they may have noticed, clothes and objects, such as watches or jewellery, which they might have come across. And in a major crime investigation the police spend a great deal of time going round houses in the vicinity of a crime scene asking people if they have seen anything suspicious, and so on. And yet witness identifications and witness descriptions are among the most inaccurate and unreliable forms of evidence the police and the courts have to deal with. Great care must be taken therefore to protect an innocent person against a false identification.

IDENTIFICATION PARADES
The Home Office has issued strict guidelines to be used in conducting identity parades. The suspect should be placed in a line-up with at least eight others, who should be of similar age, height and general appearance. He should be allowed to stand where he likes and to change his position after one witness has passed along the line. He is usually given a leaflet explaining his rights and allowed to have a solicitor present, so long as this does not cause 'unreasonable delay'.

The witness must not be allowed to see the suspect before the parade. Only one witness should walk along the line at a time and he should be told that the suspect may or may not be in the line-up. If he cannot make an identification he may be allowed to hear the participants speak or move in a specific way.

An identity parade must take precedence over identification by photographs. The witness should be shown at least twelve photographs of similar-looking people and be told that the suspect's picture may or may not be in the collection. If a firm identification is made from a photograph the witness should be asked to attend an identity parade.

REAL-LIFE EXAMPLES
● Two men broke into a bungalow at Braintree, Essex, belonging to the owner of the Barn Restaurant, which was nearby, in November, 1972. When the owner, his wife and daughter came home they were confronted by the two raiders, neither of whom was masked, but one was armed with a gun. Over 45 minutes the gunman shot dead the owner's wife, and shot and injured both the owner and his daughter. Luckily they both survived and identified George Ince as the gunman at identity parades. But he had an alibi and after two acrimonious trials was acquitted. Later, another man and his confederate admitted to the crime and were convicted.

3 IDENTIFICATION (IDENTIKIT, PHOTO-FIT AND POLICE ARTISTS)

Observability 9/10
Usefulness 4/10

IDENTIKIT
First devised by Hugh C. McDonald of the Los Angeles Police Department in the 1940s to translate witness descriptions into actual pictures of faces. It consisted of a series of line drawings of 102 pairs of eyes, 32 noses, 33 lips, 52 chins and 25 moustaches and beards, all on transparencies which could be fitted together to make a face. And because each transparency was coded it became possible to transmit a likeness over the phone by merely reading out the codes for the features used. It was introduced to Britain in the 1960s and scored some spectacular successes, like the apprehension of the murderer Edwin Bush in 1961. But it also had some failures, such as the A6 murder. The identikit pictures produced from the description furnished by Valerie Storey, who was raped after her boyfriend had been killed, and other witnesses, looked nothing like each other and did not resemble James Hanratty who was later hanged for the crime.

PHOTO-FIT
This was a development of identikit introduced in 1971, and consisted of photographic images rather than line drawings. It had 204 forehead and hairstyles, 96 pairs of eyes, 89 noses, 101 mouths, 74 chin and cheek sections and various other images such as ears, beards and moustaches, spectacles and hats and caps. More recent developments featuring computer-aided graphics technology have enabled three-dimensional images to be produced (video-fit or E-fit), with colour and texture added.

POLICE ARTISTS
The police have made use of artists, to translate witness reports into pictures of suspects, for a long time. Even before the invention of the identikit, artists were helping the police and the tradition continues to this day. Even with identikit etc., artists have often been used to add moles or other features to a face produced on transparencies. An artist can also reproduce an expression or a particular way in which facial features are set, which no mechanical method can do and, working closely with witnesses, artists have been able to produce some remarkably accurate likenesses.

REAL-LIFE EXAMPLES
● Stephanie Slater was kidnapped by Michael Sams in January, 1992. Released after a ransom had been paid she was able to describe him and freelance artist Julia Quenzler produced a very good impression. When it was shown on *Crimewatch UK* together with some voice tapes, they were easily recognised by Sam's first wife. He was arrested and later confessed to kidnapping Stephanie.

3 KNIFE WOUNDS

Observability 8/10
Usefulness 7/10

APPLICATION

These include cutting (incised) wounds or stab wounds, see also THROAT CUTTING page 67) and SHARP INSTRUMENTS (page 64). Because cuts are made with a sweeping or slashing movement, they are usually found on the unprotected parts of the body, such as the hands, arms and face. Cut-throat wounds are dealt with in the appropriate section.

The appearance of stab wounds gives information, although often not very precise information, about the weapon inflicting them. Roughening of the skin and bruising round the entry wound indicates a blunt instrument, for example a pair of scissors. The sharper the weapon, the cleaner will be the cut. But multiple stab wounds are often characterised by torn edges as the victim struggles or the knife is twisted in the body. In addition, because skin is elastic, when the blade penetrates, the skin stretches and springs back when the weapon is withdrawn. Nevertheless, the length of the entry wound is a guide to the width of the knife. A symmetrical wound with two sharp ends indicates a double edged knife, whereas if one end of the wound is blunt the knife may have only one sharp side, like a kitchen knife. The depth of penetration gives only the minimum length of the knife because it may not have gone in up to the hilt.

The angle of the wound also gives information about the person wielding the weapon. A right or left-handed assailant will produce different angles, as will a person standing in front of the victim, or standing behind but leaning over to strike from the front.

Another point to be determined is: were the wounds self-inflicted or not? A suicide, though, is usually easy to detect: the lack of defensive wounds, fingerprints on the weapon which is usually nearby, presence of a suicide note, and people who stab themselves usually lift their clothes to expose the bare skin and rarely inflict multiple wounds. Wounds to the side, back or stomach usually indicate HOMICIDE (*see* page 126) rather than suicide.

REAL-LIFE EXAMPLES

● Mrs Swift of Stockton-on Tees claimed that her husband, who had a single stab wound, had killed himself. But pathologist Sir Bernard Spilsbury showed that Patrick Swift, who was right-handed, could not have thrust the knife in at that angle.

● In the famous Wigwam Murder in 1942 Professor Keith Simpson noticed that stab wounds which Joan Woolf had suffered were made with a curious knife with a bent-over tip like a parrot's beak. It was traced to murderer August Sangret, a Canadian soldier.

3 LIVIDITY

Observability   8/10
Usefulness   6/10

Post-mortem lividity is also sometimes known as Hypostasis or Liver Mortis. After death, the blood stops circulating and sinks under gravity to the blood vessels in the lowest portion of the body. As the red blood corpuscles settle first the lowest part of the body takes on a livid colour (thus 'lividity').

The process begins immediately after death, but it takes from one to three hours for a patchy bluish-pink discoloration to appear and from six to eight hours for the colour to become continuous over a large area and even then if the skin is pressed the lividity will momentarily disappear. After ten to twelve hours the stain is permanent. Lividity cannot form where the blood capillaries are compressed, for example by the action of tight clothing or a ligature, or if the body is pressed against a hard surface. For a body which has been lying on its back on the floor, livid patches will occur at the back of the neck, in the small of the back and the backs of the thighs, not on the buttocks, shoulders or the back of the head.

APPLICATION

The onset of lividity was once one of the factors in establishing time of death, but is now very rarely so used, because of the number of factors influencing the time of formation, such as loss of blood by injury or the obesity of the corpse. Its main use to the investigator is to establish if the body has been moved sometime after death, as the pattern of lividity will establish the original position.

In some cases lividity can resemble bruising, but the difference can be established by cutting into the area of staining. Blood will drain freely from the vessels in a lividity stain, but in a bruise the blood will have drained into the surrounding tissues. This can be confirmed by examining sections of the tissues under a microscope.

REAL-LIFE EXAMPLE

● Petrus Hauptfleisch, who lived in Cape Province, South Africa, strangled his elderly mother in bed. Later he moved the body to the kitchen stove, doused it with petrol and claimed that she had been accidentally burned to death while trying to clean the stove chimney with petrol. But his story was disproved by the lividity of the body which showed it had lain on its back after death. He was hanged in Cape Town in 1926.

3 MUMMIFICATION

Observability 2/10
Usefulness 8/10

APPLICATION

Mummification is a natural process which takes place when the normal process of decomposition is interfered with, usually by the body drying out. The process was known before 3,000BC in Egypt when the skin of bodies buried in shallow graves in hot sand became dry and leathery and the body was preserved. The process can also occur in temperate climates if the body is wrapped up well and exposed to a current of warm dry air. There have been several cases where the corpses of unwanted babies wound with material and placed in drawers or cupboards have mummified. The process is helped by the fact that new-born infants have few bacteria in the gut to initiate decomposition. Adult mummification in temperate climates is not as common.

REAL-LIFE EXAMPLES

- The Rhyl mummy is mentioned elsewhere (*see* DECOMPOSITION page 79) and also the Rochdale mummy (*see* FINGERPRINTS page 84).
- A cellarman, who had been instructed to tidy up in the coal-cellar of a pub in Southwark in 1935, found a body tied up in curtain material. It was mummified. It turned out that a year before an old man mistaking the cellar door for the front door had fallen nine feet to his death. The barman, not wishing to inform the police, for reasons of his own, wrapped the body up and left it in the cellar, gave his employer notice and left. He was soon apprehended, but his story was believed and he was convicted only of concealing a body.
- In August, 1981, two workers in a peat shredding mill at Lindow Moss, Cheshire, discovered a mummified body. It was 1,000 or more years old and has since been called Lindow Man (or Pete Marsh). Probably a sacrificial victim, he had been stabbed, beaten, strangled and had his throat cut, before being thrown into the bog. The acid nature of the soil helped to preserve the body. Mummified bodies have also been found in peat bogs in Denmark and most seem to be 1,500 to 2,000 years old.

3 PAINT OR VARNISH

Observability 7/10
Usefulness 8/10

Paint or varnish on the clothing of a victim can show that they were assaulted in one location then moved to another. Paint dust in the air of a crime scene could be transferred to the clothing of a suspect. Chips of paint can also be knocked off a car or a window frame, for example, and examination of these can point to where they came from.

APPLICATION

If paint or varnish chips are large enough they can be physically matched to their source, but a more reliable method and one which also works with smaller samples of paint is to match the paint layers. An old building might have many layers of paint on its walls or woodwork and microscopic examination of a small flake will reveal the different layers which can then be compared with the suspected source. The more layers that are examined the better the chance that there will not be an accidental match.

The layers of paint on a car are strictly controlled by the makers, who usually keep records of the paints and undercoats used. Thus a specific model, so long as an owner has not repainted it, can often be identified by the system of paint layers.

Spectroscopic analysis is also useful in identifying paint samples as this can determine the constitution or composition of the paint.

REAL-LIFE EXAMPLES

● In a rape case, the perpetrator drove the victim into a wood and his car hit a branch and chipped off a small piece of paint which stuck on the bark. The paint colour was later discovered to be 'Harvest Gold', which was then traced to Austin Allegro hatchbacks made between May 1973 and August 1975. When a suspect was questioned by the police they noticed that he had an Allegro hatchback, coloured Harvest Gold, outside his London flat, and it had a chip missing from the exact height above the ground that the branch had been damaged in the wood. The man was convicted of rape.

3 PALM PRINTS, FOOTPRINTS, ETC

Observability 5/10
Usefulness 6/10

APPLICATION

Just as the ridge patterns seen in FINGERPRINTS (*see* page 84) can be used to identify individuals, so can the line patterns on the palms of the hands and even on the soles of bare feet. But they are much less useful, simply because they are less often seen than ordinary fingerprints and few collections are kept by investigatory agencies. They are also more difficult to classify. But a palm print left at the scene of the crime has just as much validity as a fingerprint.

Footprints (boot or shoe prints) and also tyre marks may also be left at the scene of a crime. These are first carefully photographed, usually with oblique lighting to give the best contrast, and a ruler placed at the side to give a measure of scale. Then a framework of card or wood is built around the impression and filled with plaster of Paris or one of the new quick-setting materials. When hardened, this can be removed and will give a permanent record of the print or tyre mark, which can be compared with the suspect's shoes, car, etc.

Tool marks can also be treated in the same way, but on a much smaller scale, and finer casting materials are used instead of plaster of Paris.

REAL-LIFE EXAMPLES

● The first time a palm print was used as evidence in a murder trial in England was in 1942, when two men, George Silverosa and Sam Dashwood, were convicted of the brutal murder of a Jewish pawnbroker in East London, by a palm print left by one of them on the inside of the robbed safe.

● Perhaps the most use ever made of palm prints was at Potter's Bar, after the golf course murder in 1955. A forty-six-year-old woman had been battered to death on the seventeenth tee with a heavy iron tee-marker, in what looked like an attempt at rape and on the metal was a partial palm print. The police undertook the mass palm printing of all the local men. Some 9,000 prints were taken, and one of them matched the print on the tee marker. It was from seventeen-year-old Michael Queripel, who was sentenced to be 'detained during Her Majesty's pleasure'.

● More recently, the Stockwell Strangler was identified in June 1986 when he left a palm print on a bathroom window he had climbed through in order to strangle the elderly lady who lived in the flat. But at the time the palm print collection at Scotland yard was not computerised and it had to be searched manually. It therefore took some time to turn up the owner, experienced burglar Kenneth Erskine, who was eventually convicted of seven murders and sentenced to at least 40 years in prison.

3 POLYGRAPH

Observability   2/10
Usefulness   3/10

APPLICATION

This is the so-called 'lie-detector', though its efficiency is open to doubt. It measures blood pressure, pulse rate, respiration and electrical skin response. These measurements are recorded by pens which run to and fro across moving strips of paper producing a wiggly line and occasional peaks. The theory is that when a person tells a lie a change occurs in one or more of these measurements, which is easily seen by the large pen movement. But they must be calibrated first, with the questioner asking normal questions of the subject, which he can answer without stress, before the more difficult ones to which the subject might lie. Even their advocates admit that polygraphs need skilled operators and in the United States, where many states use them, guidelines in their use suggest that they should not be used with the following: psychopathic liars, people who are mentally disturbed or who have served long terms of imprisonment (prisoners seem to build a resistance to polygraph testing), young children or anybody who is hungry, thirsty, emotionally upset or suffering from a number of illnesses which affect breathing, like the common cold or emphysema.

The FBI serial crime unit at Quantico, Virginia, USA, has also shown that some SERIAL KILLERS (*see* page 132) can easily fool the polygraph.

Polygraph evidence is accepted in some courts in the USA, but not in UK courts.

One of the undoubted successes of the instrument in the USA has been people's fear of it. If the police ask a suspect to take a polygraph test and he refuses it does indicate that he may have something to hide and is worthy of further investigation.

REAL-LIFE EXAMPLES

● *See* also POISONS (STREET DRUGS: AMPHETAMINES, page 61, for more on the following case. When the military police were called to the apartment of Captain Jeffrey MacDonald and his family, at Fort Bragg, North Carolina, early on the morning of Tuesday, 17 February, 1970, they found carnage inside. The captain's wife and two small children had all been beaten about the head and brutally stabbed to death and he was suffering a chest wound. He said that they had been attacked during the night by a gang of hippies. But he only had a minor wound which could well have been self-inflicted. Army investigators decided that his story was false, but MacDonald refused to take a polygraph test. He was eventually charged with murder, but it was not until 1979 that he was finally convicted and sentenced to life imprisonment.

3 POST-MORTEM (AUTOPSY) (I)

Observability   9/10
Usefulness   9/10

Post-mortem examinations, often called autopsies in America, can be of two types: the hospital or clinical post-mortem and the coroner's post-mortem. The clinical one is usually done to determine the nature of a disease from which a person has died and need not concern us further. The other, which is usually very much more extensive, is one ordered by a coroner in the case of a murder, suicide, accidental death (unless the reason for the death is obvious and there are no suspicious circumstances), the sudden death of someone in good health or death in suspicious circumstances, a prisoner who dies in custody and cases of suspected poisoning.

Often such a post-mortem will be conducted by a specialised Home Office forensic pathologist, who in the case of murder may be called in as soon as the body is found. In England and Wales there are some 50 of these pathologists. About 20 come from departments of forensic medicine at university teaching hospitals and the rest are National Health Service hospital pathologists.

APPLICATION
There are four specific things a coroner's post-mortem will try to establish:

1. Cause of death – the agent causing death, such as a knife, gun, car, poison, etc.

2. Mechanism of death – the injury to the body that caused death, such as a ruptured artery, heart seizure, etc.

3. Manner of death – was it HOMICIDE (see page 126), suicide, accidental or a natural death?

4. TIME OF DEATH (*see* page 114).

Other things which a pathologist will try to determine to help in the investigation are:
- How long did the victim live after the injury or injuries?
- Was the body left where the assault took place or moved afterwards?
- What were the relative positions of the attacker and the attacked (for example did the attacker stand behind the victim?) and is there evidence of a struggle?
- Has there been a sexual assault and can the presence of semen be established?
- Was the victim under the effects of alcohol or drugs?

3 POST-MORTEM (II) PROCEDURE   Observability   9/10
                                     Usefulness   9/10

1. The body, wrapped in a plastic sheet or body bag, is removed to the mortuary. Here the plastic sheet is carefully examined to collect any debris – HAIRS (*see* page 91), FIBRES (*see* page 83) etc. – which has fallen from the clothing.

2. The body can now be identified. This could wait, however, if there is difficulty in identification, or if the body must be cleaned up to avoid distressing relatives who have to view it.

3. Photographs are taken of the body, clothed and unclothed, which is also weighed, measured, fingerprinted and X-rayed (to determine if any bones are broken or bullets or other metal objects are inside).

4. External examination comes next. All clothing is carefully inspected. Fibre samples are taken and any stains are examined. The naked body is then carefully gone over to note any exuded material, like froth from the mouth in DROWNING (*see* page   ) cases. All wounds are studied and their locations plotted on a diagram. Scars, tattoos, moles, etc., are noted for identification purposes. At this stage, the fingernails are looked at and any debris underneath removed for examination. The hair is inspected and the skin checked for needle marks. The genitals are also inspected for signs of rape.

5. After washing the body and taking samples of hair from the eyebrows, head, facial and pubic regions, an internal examination and dissection now take place. Dissection usually begins with a large Y-shaped incision made from the two shoulders right down to the pubic region, which opens the whole of the body cavity. Blood is taken at this stage from a major vein and tested for alcohol, carbon monoxide or various other POISONS (*see* pages 34 to 63) and it can also be submitted for blood grouping (*see* also BLOOD (SEROLOGY), page 73) and DNA PROFILING (page 80). The lungs, heart, oesophagus and trachea are removed and inspected. The abdominal organs: liver, spleen, kidneys, adrenals, stomach and intestines, are next removed and also studied. Then come the pelvic organs, the bladder, uterus and ovaries. Samples of urine, cerebro-spinal fluid are taken for analysis and the contents of the stomach emptied out and collected. The partially digested food can give vital information about the time of death. *See* also TIME OF DEATH, page 114. A fine-needled syringe is used to take samples of the jelly-like fluid behind the lens of the eye. Analysis of this also helps to determine when death occurred. Bullet wounds can also be studied in more detail to determine the direction of travel of the bullets and to recover them, if possible. *See* also BALLISTICS page 70. The skull is cut away and the brain removed and examined.

6. After samples of tissue have been taken from various organs for microscopic analysis, the organs are returned to the body which is then sewn up, for subsequent burial or cremation.

3 PSYCHIC DETECTION

Observability   3/10
Usefulness   5/10

Most detectives will admit, at least privately, to a gut feeling about a case or a suspect. Sometimes it will merely be an idea that a suspect is not telling the truth; occasionally it may be a hunch that someone not apparently involved in the case *is* involved. Call it intuition or instinct or just an impression; many police officers recognise it and will tell you that it often makes the difference between just an average detective and a really good one. So it is not really surprising that policemen will sometimes listen to people who claim to be able to tell where missing property, or sometimes even missing people, are hidden, by what they claim are special psychic powers.

REAL-LIFE EXAMPLES

- A remarkable case occurred in Edmonton, Canada, in 1928. A young farm boy, Vernon Booher, shot his mother, his older brother and two farm hands. But there was nothing to connect him to the crimes, since the police could not find the murder weapon. They called in psychic specialist, Dr Maximilian Langsner. He claimed to be able to read the mind of a criminal and after attending the inquest soon led the policemen to the hiding place of the rifle, near the farm house. Then, after Dr Langsner had sat outside his cell for an hour without speaking to him, Vernon Booher confessed to all the murders. But at his trial the defence contended that the confession had been obtained after Dr Langsner had hypnotised the farm-hand. The confession was subsequently thrown out. At a subsequent trial the governor of the prison where Booher had been held said that Booher had confessed to him even before he had met Dr Langsner. Booher was convicted and hanged.
- Peter Hurkos, a Dutchman, who was said to have remarkable powers, was asked by the Boston police to help in the search for the Boston Strangler (Boston, USA, 1962 – 1964). He examined scarves and nylon stockings used by the sex killer to strangle his thirteen victims and studied police photographs by laying them face-down on the desk and passing his hands over them. Then he led the police to a known sex-offender, who, as a result, voluntarily entered the state mental hospital. The killings stopped, but several months later a woman was sexually attacked in her home, though not murdered. From the description she gave of her attacker, Albert DeSalvo was arrested, but then judged to be a schizophrenic and not fit to stand trial. While he was in a mental hospital he confessed to all the murders and, though never charged, was regarded by most authorities as being the most likely candidate for being the Boston Strangler. He was imprisoned for sex offences committed before the stranglings and was later killed in prison by a fellow inmate.

3 RIGOR MORTIS   Observability 6/10
                       Usefulness   5/10

This is the extreme stiffness of a dead body. Normally it comes on two to four hours after death and can last for up to four days. Rigidity usually starts in the jaw and neck and proceeds down the body to the feet. The reason for rigor mortis is the disappearance in the body after death of the chemical required for muscle contraction, adenosine triphosphate (ATP). When the ATP has completely gone the muscle becomes rigid and remains in that condition until decomposition begins.

If there has been a violent struggle before death, or death has occurred by electrocution, in which the muscles are stimulated, the ATP will have been used up and rigor mortis will come on more quickly. Death by CARBON MONOXIDE poisoning (*see* page 47), in contrast, will result in little loss of ATP and rigor mortis will be delayed.

APPLICATION
Rigor Mortis is one of the indicators of TIME OF DEATH (*see* page 114), but it is not a particularly good one because of the large number of variables involved. It is affected by weight. Very fat and heavy people may never develop it at all, while with thin people and children it comes on more rapidly. The temperature of the surroundings also makes a difference. A high temperature speeds up the process, while cold slows it down. This is a device which has been used by crime-writers in the past, cooling the body artificially to make it appear that death has occurred before it actually has.

REAL-LIFE EXAMPLES
● Pathologist Professor Keith Simpson quotes a case in his book *Forty Years Of Murder*, which he solved over the phone! He was rung up at his home in London by the police in Guernsey who wanted him to come and assist them in an investigation they were making into the death of a teenaged boy. The parents said they had gone out for the evening and arrived home at about 11.30 to find their son dead and covered in blood. The local doctor examined the boy at 1.30 in the morning and found rigor mortis so well established that he estimated the teenager had been dead six or seven hours. This would have meant that he died while his parents were still at home. Simpson asked the police to get the temperature of the body. This indicated that the death probably took place at about 11 at night, and thus the parents were off the hook. It turned out that the boy had got drunk on his father's whisky, dropped the beaker and badly cut his foot on the broken glass. He died of shock and loss of blood and the rigor mortis was really a kind of cadaveric spasm brought on by fear and panic.

3 SCENES OF CRIMES PROCEDURES

Observability 8/10
Usefulness 9/10

What happens at the scene of a crime, at the beginning, can literally, make or break the investigation. *See* also POLICE PROCEDURE (MECHANICS OF A MURDER INVESTIGATION, page 135).

APPLICATION

The job of the first police officer on the scene of a major crime, usually a beat or mobile uniformed officer, is to 'secure the scene', that is to keep people from trampling on possible clues, etc. Eventually, this will be done by setting a boundary of brightly coloured tape round the area. The officer then calls for reinforcements, an ambulance or further officers or both. Assistance will be given to injured persons and, if they are found hanging, they should be cut down and artificial respiration administered.

If the person is obviously dead, then the body must not be moved until examined and photographed.

The whole scene is photographed. These days, it is usually videotaped as well. Many still photographs will be taken of the body, if there is one, and of the room or area where it was found. These will be used in the investigation, for information, for refreshing people's memories and for use in court.

Sketch plans are also made of the scene, the position of the body is recorded and the location of objects in the room or external features (if outside) are placed on the plan.

Medical assistance is required to establish if the victim is dead and to estimate the TIME OF DEATH (see page 114). *See* also POST-MORTEM (pages 102, 103), etc.

The so-called fingertip searches are performed, often by specialised officers, to collect any evidence which will help in the investigation. And the scene is also examined for fingerprints.

REAL-LIFE EXAMPLES

● Arthur Hutchins broke into a house in Sheffield in October, 1983, and stabbed to death the father, mother and son he found sleeping there and raped the younger daughter at knife-point. He later denied being at the house, but his palm prints were found, together with some of his very rare blood and his teeth-marks on a piece of cheese. At his trial the jury were shown part of a police-made video showing the body of the father lying on the stairs. It was the first time such evidence had been presented in a British court. The jury asked to see the whole video showing all the victims' injuries and were cautioned by the judge not to allow themselves to be influenced by the horror of the video. They nevertheless brought in guilty verdicts against Hutchinson.

3 SCHIZOPHRENIA
Observability 3/10
Usefulness 6/10

The commonest of all forms of insanity, it is experienced by one person in a hundred; *see* also FORENSIC PSYCHIATRY (page 87). Schizophrenia is the general term for a group of psychotic illnesses characterised by disturbances in emotional reaction, behaviour and thought processes. Called sometimes 'split personality', the term refers to the fact that the sufferer's thoughts and feelings do not relate to each other logically. When the subject appears to have more than one personality, it is called Multiple Personality Disorder.

APPLICATION
No single cause has been identified for schizophrenia. Hereditary factors may play some part, as may severe stress and a chemical imbalance may also be a contributing cause since it is known that AMPHETAMINES (*see* page 61) can cause a schizophrenic illness. Symptoms usually occur between the ages of 15 and 30 for men and about five years later for women. The sufferer becomes progressively more withdrawn and introverted and may suffer delusions (false ideas which do not respond to logical argument) and sometimes hallucinations (sensory experiences which have no external stimuli). The victim can hear voices telling him or her to do things, which may be criminal acts, and feelings of hostility and persecution are not uncommon.

Electrical shock treatment used to be popular, but today treatment is mainly by the use of antipsychotic drugs and psychotherapy.

Schizophrenics may be treated initially in hospitals, but most return to the community once the major symptoms are controlled. Some 90 per cent of sufferers can return to some degree of independence and many will live normal lives, provided they keep up their medication.

REAL-LIFE EXAMPLES
● Many murderers in the past have been diagnosed as schizophrenics, though not all have passed the insanity test of the McNaghten Rules; *see* FORENSIC PSYCHIATRY (page 87).
● Peter Sutcliffe, the Yorkshire Ripper, was interviewed by many psychiatrists, for both the defence and the prosecution, before his trial and all diagnosed him as being a paranoid schizophrenic. But the trial judge refused to allow Sutcliffe to plead guilty to the lower charge of manslaughter due to diminished responsibility (*see* MANSLAUGHTER page 130), which would have confined him in a mental institution, and insisted on a trial for murder. Sutcliffe was duly convicted of murder and jailed for life with the recommendation that he serve at least 30 years. Three years later he was again diagnosed as a schizophrenic and moved to Broadmoor Mental Hospital where he currently resides.

3 SEMEN

Observability 5/10
Usefulness 8/10

Semen is of great importance forensically if left at the scene of the crime or in the body of a victim.

APPLICATION

The use is mainly in rape or sexual assault cases, but since these are occasionally associated with MURDER (*see* page 133), it can have a wider application.

Semen stains will occur on clothes, bed clothes, furniture and carpets, and also on and in the body of a victim. In the collection for examination the stains are normally left to dry in the air, covered with a clean sheet of paper and, where convenient, placed in a container. This is usually a paper bag, not a plastic one since plastic bags prevent drying out, leading to deterioration of the sample. If wet, the stains may yield enough liquid for sampling separately in bottles or jars and semen left on or in the victim will be swabbed or washed off. If the stain is not visible it can be detected under Ultra-Violet light when it will fluoresce, but care must be taken since other body fluids, such as urine, also fluoresce. Under a microscope semen can be identified by the spermatocytes. In one ejaculation there may be more than a hundred million spermatocytes. But sperm cells are not always visible, as in men who have undergone a vasectomy, or have a very low sperm count, or who produce none at all. In this case, semen can be detected by the acid phosphatase test, although experience is needed in using it as other bodily fluids can also give a positive reaction.

Some 80 per cent of males are 'secretors', that is, their blood group can be determined from their semen, though the specificity of the test is not as good as those used on ordinary blood. But this has been largely superseded by DNA PROFILING (*see* page 80), which can be done on semen and offers the possibility of individual identification.

REAL-LIFE EXAMPLES

● Andrei Chikatilo, the Russian serial-killer, was arrested by the police in September 1984, when he was observed trying to pick up young people at a railway station in Rostov. By this time he had already claimed more than thirty victims. His blood tested group A. But the profile the police had put together of the serial-killer included a blood group based on semen left on one of his victims, and that was group AB. The Russian scientists did not realise at the time that there were non-secretors, men whose semen did not match with their blood groups, and DNA testing was not then available. Chikatilo was released. He went on to murder at least another fourteen young people before being finally captured in November, 1990.

3 SEX CRIMES   Observability 5/10
                                    Usefulness   6/10

While sexual intercourse is often associated with SERIAL KILLERS (*see* page 132), it does not appear an essential factor in the process. In addition, criminologists regard the sex act, if it occurs at all, as an unimportant part of the sex crime. As a multiple rapist confessed to a FBI investigator: 'Rape is the least enjoyable part of the entire crime'. Domination and humiliation are far more important to the perpetrator than the enjoyment of sexual intimacies.

Violence is another essential component of the act. In extreme cases there may be a frenzied attack and instead of actual sex the sex organs may be mutilated. It has also been postulated that sex crimes are the province of weak and often impotent men who cannot exert themselves sufficiently in ordinary society; *see* also SERIAL KILLERS, page 132.

REAL-LIFE EXAMPLES
● Sutcliffe, the Yorkshire Ripper, was said to be goaded by his impotence and John Christie, of 10 Rillington Place infamy, was incapable of sex with women who were conscious or even alive.
● Chikatilo, the Russian serial killer, could only achieve an erection during a frenzy of blood letting and Douglas Clark, the Hollywood Sunset Strip killer, kept the severed head of one of his victims so that he could make it up afterwards and use it in sex acts.
● There appear to be some exceptions to this generalisation, however. Ted Bundy had 19 known victims and probably many more. All were young women and some teenaged girls. He was a handsome man whose charm and wit made him very attractive to women, as evidenced by his string of girl friends. He was awarded a scholarship in Chinese studies at Stanford University in 1972 and later received a degree in psychology. He worked as an assistant director for the Seattle crime commission and later was accepted by the University of Utah to study law. A man clearly with achievements and gifts most men would envy, and the opportunity for sexual recreation any time he felt like it, yet he had this compulsion to rape and murder young women, which eventually led him to the electric chair in Florida.
● In 1979, Randy Kraft was a 35-year-old successful computer consultant in California, who owned his own house, which he shared with his homosexual lover, and was regarded as gentle and mild-mannered. Yet in 1983 he was convicted of 16 homosexual murders, and widely suspected of having committed many more, and most of his young male victims were horrifically tortured before death. His lover knew nothing of his crimes.

3 SEX CRIMES (INVESTIGATION)

Observability 7/10
Usefulness 8/10

APPLICATION

See also SCENE OF CRIME PROCEDURES (page 106). In a sex crime, the investigator will look for evidence of a struggle, what type of weapon was used – if any – and how the victim and assailant actually reached the scene of the crime. Did they walk, for example, or come by car, etc.?

In addition to photographing the crime scene, particular attention will be paid to the victim's injuries, photographing these with a ruler placed beside each one to give perspective and scale. The doctor will examine the victim and collect samples from the vagina, in the case of a female, anus, mouth and throat, for the presence of sperm. Seminal stains are of course crucial evidence that a sexual attack has taken place and these may be found on the victim's clothes, bed linen and towels, paper tissues, furniture etc. If a female, the victim's pubic hair will be combed for evidence of hair left by the attacker, and samples of the victim's pubic hair and other body hair will be taken in case some has been transferred to the attacker or his clothes.

Bloodstained material is collected and any liquid or dried blood which can be found on or near the victim. A sample of the victim's blood will also be used as a control.

Saliva samples will be taken from the victim and the victim's body swabbed to collect saliva samples from the assailant. Seminal samples, saliva and blood may all be submitted for DNA analysis.

If a suspect is arrested, his clothing will be examined for evidence, such as HAIR (*see* page 91), FIBRES (*see* page 83) and BLOOD (*see* page 73), from the victim and for semen stains. His pubic hair will be examined for the presence of the victim's hair and samples of his pubic hair and other body hair will be taken to compare with samples from the victim. The suspect's hair can also be used for DNA analysis, *see* page 80.

REAL-LIFE EXAMPLES

● Neville Heath was a blond, good-looking young ex-bomber pilot who was known for his ability to charm women. In June 1946 he took a female acquaintance into a hotel room in Notting Hill late one night, thrashed her with a metal-tipped whip, horribly sexually mutilated her body and suffocated her. With the arrogance characteristic of many murderers he got in touch with the police and was eventually detained. A bloodstained scarf was found in his possession and a riding whip of a particular leather cross-weave which fitted exactly marks made on the victim's body. He was convicted and hanged.

3 SKELETONS
Observability   6/10
Usefulness   7/10

APPLICATION

Starting with a collection of bones the investigator is faced with two questions: are they human? and if they are, how many people do they belong to? The expert anatomist can usually answer the first, though sometimes the precipitin test may be necessary. The second question involves the tedious job of putting the bones together to make more or less complete skeletons.

The next problem is to establish the sex, age, height and any other characteristics which will help in identification. Sex can be determined relatively easily from adult skeletons. The pelvic bones in the female correspond to wider hips than the male and the ratio of the length of two bones (the ischium-pubis index) helps to distinguish female from male. With children before puberty the problem is more difficult there being very little difference between the two.

Age can be determined by looking at the SKULL (*see* page 112), teeth and centres of ossification, which tend to fill out and fuse together as a child grows, giving the bones their final shape and size. And a skilled anatomist can estimate age, particularly with younger people, often to within a year or two. Examination of the growing ends of bones can give remarkably precise estimates of age up to 25. After that age, determination is a matter of examining the changes undergone by the skull and other bones.

The height of a person can be deduced from the length of the long bones, in the arms and legs. Various formulae are available. Professor Keith Simpson applied Pearson's formula in 1942 (now superseded by the Dapertuis and Hadden formula) to a single bone available to him in the Dobson case and came up with an estimate of 5 feet $1/2$ inch, which turned out to be very close to the truth.

REAL-LIFE EXAMPLES

● Pathologist Sir Sidney Smith describes a case, in *Mostly Murder*, which he worked on in Cairo, during the 1920s. A parcel containing three bones, which had been found at the bottom of a well, was delivered to his office. After examining them he told the police. "They are the bones of a slim young woman, who was between 23 and 25 when she died, which was at least three months ago. She had probably had at least one pregnancy, perhaps more. Her left leg was shorter than the right and she walked with a pronounced limp. Probably she had polio when a child. She was killed by a shotgun loaded with home-made slugs, fired in an upward direction from a range of about three yards. The killer was standing or sitting in front and slightly to her left. She was not killed outright, but died about seven to ten days later, probably from septic peritonitis due to the shooting." How did he do it? Read his book!

3 SKULLS
Observability 5/10
Usefulness 8/10

Skulls have long been a potent symbol of death, the 'skull and crossed bones' on the pirate's flag and on poison bottles being emotive examples. But there is a surprising amount of information which may be obtained from skulls.

APPLICATION

They are often classified by their cephalic index; the ratio of the maximum width to the maximum length. The higher the index the more spherical in shape is the skull. Age can be estimated approximately by the state of sutures on the skull. The vault of the cranium consists of a number of bones which join at their edges more or less closely in so-called sutures. In children, there are large gaps between the bones which begin to close up after the age of 30 and it is from these that age can be estimated.

There are also significant differences between male and female skulls. Male bones are usually larger and a male skull is usually bigger. The jawbone is heavier and more pointed than a female jaw, which has a more rounded shape. The nasal aperture of a man tends to be long and narrow and in the shape of a tear-drop while the female skull has a more pear-shaped opening. The sockets in the skull holding the eyes, the orbits, are much more rounded in a female whereas in a male they are more rectangular. A woman's forehead, too, is more upright than a man's which slopes back more and has a pronounced brow ridge over the eyes.

REAL-LIFE EXAMPLES

● In September, 1935, the remains of two dismembered bodies were discovered in a ravine near Moffat, Scotland. The killer had gone to considerable lengths to make the remains unidentifiable. The ears, eyes, noses, lips and skin of the faces had been removed. Teeth had been extracted and fingers removed to prevent fingerprint identification. But a portion of a body had been wrapped in an edition of the *Sunday Graphic* newspaper which was traced to Lancaster and police investigations turned up the fact that two women had recently disappeared from there, the wife of a Dr Buck Ruxton and the couple's maid. Painstaking work by Professor John Glaister of Edinburgh University's Forensic Science Department and Professor J. C. Brash of Glasgow University finally conclusively identified the remains as those of the missing two women. During the investigation, they developed a startling new technique. The negative from a portrait photograph of Mrs Buxton was enlarged to life-size and an X-ray photograph of one of the skulls superimposed upon it. They made a perfect fit and thus the skull was identified as belonging to her. Dr Ruxton was convicted of the murder of both women.

3 STOMACH CONTENTS   Observability 6/10
                            Usefulness 8/10

Examination of the contents of the stomach forms part of the POST-MORTEM PROCEDURE (*see* page 103) and can give valuable information about the TIME OF DEATH (*see* page 114)

APPLICATION

After a meal is eaten the food travels into the stomach. Here it is partially digested and then passed into the small intestine. This process takes from three-and-a half to four-and-a-half hours, depending on the constitution of the food. By knowing the time of the last meal and examining the stomach contents it is thus possible to estimate the time of death. But this is only a rough guide. Physical or emotional states of the body can effect the rate of digestion and the time that food takes to pass from the stomach. A badly frightened child, for example will often vomit the stomach contents and with many people a prolonged emotional disturbance will slow down the rate of passage of food from the stomach.

REAL-LIFE EXAMPLES

● At 5.30 p.m. on 9 June, 1959, twelve-year-old Lynne Harper, the daughter of a Canadian Air Force officer, had a meal of turkey, vegetables and pineapple cake, with her parents at their home near Goderich, Ontario. She went out soon afterwards and was seen with 14 year-old Steven Truscott at 7.00 p.m. The next morning her body was found in a nearby copse. She had been raped and strangled. Steven Truscott was arrested. He had been seen alone at 8.00 p.m. and the pathologist estimated, from the contents of Lynne's stomach, that she had died not later than two hours after her meal. He had a sore penis, consistent with rape and he had grass stains on his knees. But much of the evidence against him was not strong. He didn't improve his case however by telling an incredible tale of Lynne having left him to hitch a lift in an unknown car. At his trial he was convicted of murder and sentenced to death, later commuted to life imprisonment. The conviction and sentence raised a storm of protest. Several books were written about the case and an appeal was lodged in 1967. Internationally famous pathologists, Dr Milton Helpern of New York and Professors Keith Simpson and Francis Camps from London, were asked to testify. If it could be shown that the digestion process had been slowed down, perhaps by the emotional trauma, and Lynne had died after 8.00 p.m., then it would help Steven Truscott's cause. But both Helpern and Simpson supported the conclusions of the original pathologist and Truscott's appeal was rejected. He went back to prison, but was released in 1969.

3 TIME OF DEATH

Observability 9/10
Usefulness 8/10

There are two important times associated with violent death; the legal time of death and the estimated time of death. The legal time is when it is first pronounced that death has occurred, for example when the body is discovered and a doctor officially states that the person is dead. The estimated time of death is the time when the person actually died. There may of course be a considerable difference between the two. But the important one for crime writers is the estimated time of death as this is the one which affects the investigation

APPLICATION

There are three main sources of information:

1. Witnesses who can give the time of death.
2. Post-mortem changes in the body. *See* also, POST-MORTEM (pages 102 and 103)
3. Markers found at the scene of the death, such as newspapers, letters, etc., which can help to pin down the date and so on.

Some post-mortem changes are described under LIVIDITY (*see* page 97) and RIGOR MORTIS (*see* page 105). Time of death is also discussed in FORENSIC ENTOMOLOGY (*see* page 85).

In addition, the body temperature can be used to estimate time of death. After death the body begins to cool. At the murder scene, the pathologist will note the temperature of the air and surroundings and take the rectal or vaginal temperature of the body using a special low-reading thermometer. Subtracting the rectal temperature from the normal body temperature (98.4F) and dividing by 1.5F (the rate of drop of temperature per hour) gives the approximate number of hours since death. Another method is to measure the potassium content of the fluid in the eye. When red blood-cells break down after death, potassium is released at a slow but steady rate and the increase in potassium gives a measure of the time of death. This method works only when the temperature of the body has fallen to the outside temperature.

REAL-LIFE EXAMPLES
● Neville Heath's first victim was a young woman whom he severely beat, mutilated and suffocated to death in a room of the Pembridge Court Hotel in Notting Hill, in June 1946. Pathologist Keith Simpson examined the body at 6.30 p.m. and from the vaginal temperature she looked to have been dead for ten hours, which would have put her death at 8.30 in the morning. But Simpson knew that asphyxia causes a rise in temperature of the body and, making the approximate adjustments, came up with a time of around 12 midnight. This fitted in with the time that Heath was known to have arrived at the hotel with his victim, who no doubt had been killed soon after.

3 VOICE PRINTS
Observability 4/10
Usefulness 6/10

Most people can recognise a wide variety of voices, provided they are not too distorted, and there has always been a great potential for putting this on an instrumental basis so that the recording of a voice could be used like a FINGERPRINT (*see* page 84) for establishing identity.

APPLICATION

The early work on this technique was done by the American scientist Lawrence G. Kersta who produced his voice spectrograph in 1963. Modern machines work on the same principle of recording the human voice, then scanning the recording electronically to measure either the frequency or the intensity of the sound. Only selected common words, such as 'a', 'and', 'me', 'you', etc., are used and the frequency of the sound is plotted against time to give a voice print. One of the commonest is the 'contour voice print' where points of equal frequency are connected by a contour line, producing diagrams which have wide variations for different speakers saying the same word. Attempts to disguise the voice do not affect the inherent quality, which appears in the voice print.

The technique has been accepted in some courts in the USA, but not in all and it has not been used very much by British police forces. Its potential uses are in identifying callers in phoned messages from kidnappers, in bomb-threat calls, obscene telephone calls and in voice communications by criminals to newspapers and the police.

Voice recognition methods are being used in some security installations. An operative repeats several words which must be recognised by a computer before a door can be opened.

There are also voice analysers on the market which, like a POLYGRAPH (*see* page 101) are supposed to recognise when a subject is lying. These operate by detecting very small tremors of speech and are said to work on telephone conversations, live or recorded, and of course do not need the subject to be connected to the apparatus as the polygraph does.

REAL-LIFE EXAMPLES
● Some of the drawbacks of identification by voice were shown in the Yorkshire Ripper investigation. An audio tape was sent to the police, in June 1979, after the eleventh murder, in which the speaker identified himself as the murderer. The police believed it and began looking for a man with the caller's distinctive Wearside accent, ignoring all who did not speak like him. This had disastrous consequences for the investigation, since the tape was a hoax, and it may have led indirectly to the subsequent death of further victims, before the real Yorkshire Ripper was arrested in 1981.

CHAPTER 4

OTHER ASPECTS OF CRIME – INTRODUCTION

This chapter deals with aspects of crime not covered by the others. It includes the different types of MURDER (*see* also page 133),and its near relatives, and the way in which a death is handled legally. There are also entries describing how courts and the legal system works. Laws and legal procedures vary widely, however, in different countries – even Scottish law can be very different to English – and unless it is otherwise stated what follows applies only to England and Wales. It may seem that the workings of the legal system would have little relevance for the writer of crime novels, unless they intended to write a court drama, but in real life how a court works to a large extent determines how a detective operates. The way evidence is collected and the way the police approach suspects can play a vital part in subsequent court proceedings. And it's not much good detecting the criminal if the investigator doesn't have a good chance of getting a guilty verdict from the jury.

How police forces are managed and how they operate is another part of this chapter. Even if you are not writing a police procedural you need to know what goes on in an investigation otherwise your account will not have the essential ring of truth. We have all read village whodunits where the village bobby wanders around and questions people, with not a sign of the press or his superior officers appearing on the horizon, and eventually solves the murder. Thankfully, very few people today think that it actually happens like that. But the details of who actually does what are still important and useful to know. If you are writing a police procedural, of course you may need to know considerably more about police forces, such as their conditions of work, pension schemes, etc. which are beyond the scope of this book. Useful information about your local police force: the structure of the force, where the headquarters and police stations are, the number and type of crimes committed in your area, can be obtained from the Chief Constable's Annual Report, copies of which will usually be held in your local library.

As the entries vary so much in content I have not split the pages into sections, such as APPLICATIONS, as I did in chapter 3, although I have included REAL-LIFE EXAMPLES where appropriate. I have not attempted a box system at the top of the page either, for the same reason.

4 CHILD MURDER

The vast majority of children who are murdered are killed by their parents or a close relative (*see* also INFANTICIDE page 127). Tensions in the home may spill over into violence and a defenceless child is an easy target. They can also become the victims of sexual abuse.

The murder of children by strangers is thankfully quite rare, but becoming more common. With the greater mobility of people these days the chance of young children meeting strangers is increased and some child murderers have been able to entice children into cars. Serial killing of children is much rarer still, but it has occurred.

School classrooms also seem to be becoming the target of MASS KILLERS (*see* page 131).

Kidnapping children for ransom is rather less common now than it used to be, but it can lead to murder and the past has yielded some well publicised cases, such as the Charley Ross kidnapping, Pennsylvania, USA, 1874, the Lindbergh case, New Jersey, USA (1932-4) and the kidnapping and murder of Graeme Thorne in Sidney, Australia in June 1960.

The killing of children by children is not as rare as might be supposed. Since 1748 there have been 32 killings by children under the age of 14 and 23 of them were committed in this century. Two cases have occurred in the 1990s, not counting the murder of little Jamie Bulger, which occurred in February, 1993. Many people will remember the horrifying crimes of Mary Bell, in Newcastle in 1968. She killed two children, one four and the other three and she was 11 years old at the time.

REAL-LIFE EXAMPLES
● Between July, 1982, when 11-year-old Susan Maxwell disappeared, and July 1990, when an alert gardener saw what he thought was a van driver abducting a young girl and alerted the police, Robert Black abducted and murdered at least three young girls and possibly many more. He was convicted of three murders and three kidnappings in April, 1994.
● Wayne B. Williams was convicted of the murder of two youths in Atlanta, Georgia, in February, 1982, but was widely suspected of killing 26 more teenaged children of both sexes in the period July 1979 to May 1981.

4 CONFESSIONS

There are a number of reasons why people confess to crimes. The obvious one is that they realise there is so much evidence against them that they decide to tell the truth and so ease their burden of guilt. Young and inexperienced people, or those with weak characters who are easily influenced, can sometimes be persuaded to confess to crimes, even MURDER (*see* page 133), which they have not committed. Then, experienced criminals sometimes confess in the hope that they will receive a lighter sentence and murderers sometimes confess that the killing was accidental or not premeditated in order that the charge can be reduced to MANSLAUGHTER (*see* page 130), which carries a shorter term of imprisonment. False confessions are also common in spectacular and well-publicised crimes. The Black Dahlia murder in Los Angeles in 1947, a particularly horrific crime, produced many false confessions although no-one was eventually even brought to trial.

Corroboration must therefore be sought immediately someone confesses to a crime. And the police often ask seemingly irrelevant questions in order to produce answers which can be checked.

It is also important to demonstrate that the confession was not obtained by undue pressure or inducements and it should be clearly stated if the confession was produced by the accused answering specific questions, as many are, or if he simply sat down and wrote it out himself. *See* also POLICE AND CRIMINAL EVIDENCE ACT (page 136). It is also becoming increasingly necessary to show that the confession was not obtained by infringing a person's basic human rights or by tricking them. In many states in the USA, if it can be shown that the confession was not obtained properly, the confession itself is not admissible in court and any information obtained from it, such as the location of the weapon used, etc., is not allowed either.

REAL-LIFE EXAMPLES
● Colin Stagg was arrested in August, 1993, and charged with the murder of Rachel Nickell on Wimbledon Common, a remarkably horrible crime, the year before. But before the trial began in September, 1994, Stagg's counsel objected that a large proportion of the prosecution evidence had been obtained by a police 'sting' operation. This had been conducted by an undercover policewoman, working under orders from a psychologist. She had become very friendly with Stagg and pornographic letters and tapes had been sent to encourage him to develop sexual fantasies in connection with the murder. The judge agreed that the material was inadmissible because of the way it had been obtained and the prosecution offered no further evidence. Colin Stagg was declared not guilty and released.

4 CONSPIRACY TO MURDER

A conspiracy is an agreement between two or more people to commit a crime. Any person who conspires to commit MURDER *(see* also page 133), or who solicits, proposes, encourages or persuades another to carry out a murder is also liable to be charged with the crime even though they didn't actually kill anybody.

Perhaps the most common type of conspiracy is that of two lovers who find that the spouse of one is an impediment to their being together and decide to kill the person standing in their way. Closely allied to this type is the contract killing, where the lovers pay a hitman (or woman) to do the job.

REAL-LIFE EXAMPLES

● Barbara Finch, the wife of California doctor Bernard Finch was killed by her husband and his lover, Carole Tregoff, in 1959. Both were subsequently sentenced to life imprisonment.

● Finch and Tregoff tried to find a hitman to kill Mrs Finch, before doing it themselves. A variation on this theme is the case of Kathleen Calhaem. She was in love with solicitor Kenneth Pigot, who was separated from his wife, but Pigot already had one lover. Calhaem hired a part-time private detective, then persuaded him to kill Pigot's lover. Both Calhaem and the detective were convicted of murder.

● Contract killing need have nothing to do with love. Joseph Peel was a judge in West Palm Beach, Florida and was about to be impeached by his superior, Judge Curtis Chillingworth – because of irregularities in his law practice – which would have ended his career as a lawyer. He hired two men to take the elderly judge and his wife out to sea in a small boat and drop them over the side. One of the men eventually testified against the others and Judge Peel and the other man were convicted of murder.

● In a reversal of roles 27-year-old Maria Ngarimu, who was the daughter of a Maori chieftain and held degrees in Mathematics and Chemistry, put four bullets into a roofing contractor as he spoke on the phone in the corridor of the Royal Free Hospital in Hampstead in May, 1992. The police soon charged the roofing contractor's business partner, Paul Tubbs, and employee Deith Bridges, who was a New Zealander, with the murder. But who had pulled the trigger remained a mystery. Then Ngarimu, who had gone back to New Zealand, became a born-again Christian, came to England and confessed. All three were jailed for life.

4 CORONER

A very ancient Crown office, but today in England a coroner is appointed by a county council. He is appointed for life and must be a barrister, solicitor, or medical practitioner with at least five years professional experience. His main job is to enquire into suspicious deaths and for the inquest he is assisted by a jury of between seven and eleven persons, evidence is taken on oath and expert and other witnesses may be summoned.

The inquest is convened soon after the death has been reported to the coroner and evidence of identity is given. The inquest is usually then adjourned to allow the police to make further enquiries and reconvened at a later date. It is the duty of the jury to establish how, when and where the death occurred. And until 1978 it was also their duty to say who was to be charged with MURDER (*see* page 133), MAN-SLAUGHTER (*see* page 130) or INFANTICIDE (*see* page 127).

Cases which require an inquest include murder, manslaughter or infanticide; where the death occurred in prison or was caused by a vehicle on a public highway.

Every death must be certified by a doctor and then reported to the local registrar of births, marriages and deaths, who will inform the coroner if there is anything suspicious about it. The doctor may also inform the coroner, especially if the death was sudden and unexpected and if the doctor had not seen the patient for 14 days before the death. Also to be reported are deaths during abortion, under anaesthetic or any drug-related death and deaths during operations.

The coroner is informed about deaths arising from starvation or neglect, and industrial diseases and, of course, any apparent suicides. All poisoning cases are reported, as are deaths from septicaemia, if this arose from an injury, and still-births if there is any suspicion attached to the birth.

The duties of a coroner are performed by the procurator-fiscal in Scotland. In the USA the coroner was traditionally an elected office with no qualifications required, other than not being an ex-convict, but many states have replaced this by the medical examiners office, where the officer is usually a pathologist.

REAL-LIFE EXAMPLES

● In 1929, an American actor, Philip Yale Drew, performing in Reading, was a witness at the inquest into a particularly brutal murder of a shopkeeper. He was never charged, but underwent effectively trial by inquest. However the jury finally brought in a verdict of murder against person or persons unknown and he was released from his torment. The case raised a storm of protest and today the coroner can no longer effectively try anyone. The last person named by the jury as a murderer was Lord Lucan, for the murder of Sandra Rivett in June 1975.

4 CORPUS DELICTI

The fact that no court case can proceed without a *corpus delicti* has led many people, including some murderers, to believe that no body means no case. But this is not so. *Corpus* does indeed mean 'body', but not a human body. It refers to the 'body of the crime'. In the case of MURDER (*see* page 133) it must be shown that someone has been killed, that the person missing is the one who has been done to death and that the killing was unlawful. In other words, the term refers to the actual facts of the case.

REAL LIFE EXAMPLES

● John Haigh boldly claimed: 'I have destroyed Mrs Durand-Deacon with acid. Every trace has gone. How can you prove murder if there is no body?' But he was wrong. There were traces left and he was convicted of her murder.

● James Camb also thought that he was home and dry when he pushed Gay Gibson out of the porthole of the *Durban Castle* in the middle of the Atlantic Ocean. Her body was never found either. But there were urine stains on her bed and traces of blood-streaked saliva, all indicative of strangulation. There were scratches on his arms and he had been seen in her cabin after a disturbance. Enough circumstantial evidence to make him admit pushing her out of the porthole, although he claimed it was after she was dead and that her death was accidental.

● The disappearance of Polish immigrant Stanislaw Sykut from a remote farm in Carmarthenshire in 1953 was much more difficult to investigate. The only traces found were some minute blood splashes in the farmhouse kitchen. But his business partner, Michael Onufrejczyk, who also lived at the farm, was known to have quarrelled with him and Onufrejczyk claimed that he had bought out the missing man, who had gone back to Poland. But the person he said he had borrowed the money from denied that she had lent him any, and other lies went against him at his trial. He was convicted of murder.

● A more recent case involved top civil servant, and friend of Princess Margaret, Dr Donald Hamilton, who disappeared from the flat in Brixton he shared with his male lover Kingsley Rotardier in 1985. No trace of Dr Hamilton has ever been found and it was simply by showing that Rotardier's story that Hamilton had gone abroad was a series of lies and that letters he had supposedly sent back were fakes that the police were able to build up a circumstantial case against him. The jury were convinced and Rotardier was convicted of murder.

4 CRIME PASSIONEL

A French term which means 'crime of passion' and is recognised in that country as a valid defence to a MURDER (*see* page 133) which is committed in a moment of passion – usually when one of the marriage partners discovers that they have been supplanted by another.

REAL LIFE EXAMPLES

● The idea of crime passionel has never been enshrined in English law, and this is illustrated by the two cases of Pauline Dubuisson and Ruth Ellis. Pauline Dubuisson shot and killed her lover in Paris in 1951 and was found guilty of murder without premeditation (similar to the English manslaughter verdict). See also MANSLAUGHTER (page 130). She escaped the death penalty. Ruth Ellis who also shot her lover in London in 1955 in similar circumstances was not so lucky. She was hanged.

● But in these days of rather more relaxed morals it is certainly the case that some British courts have recently looked more favourably on crimes arising from the passions of love.

● Christine Dryland, the wife of an army major serving in Germany, killed his mistress by repeatedly driving her car over her in a car park near Hanover. She was tried by a British courts martial in 1992, near Bremen, and allowed to plead not guilty to murder, but guilty to manslaughter by reason of diminished responsibility (*see* also INSANITY (page 87). She could have received a prison sentence, but instead was ordered to undergo twelve months psychiatric treatment at a London hospital, concurrent with a one-year Rhine Army probation order.

● Susan Christie was serving with the army in Northern Ireland when she met Captain Duncan McAllister. They became lovers, but he subsequently refused to leave his wife Penny, and in March 1991 Susan cut Penny's throat. At her trial, in a criminal court, she too offered a plea of guilty of manslaughter by reason of diminished responsibility, but the prosecution would not accept this. However, at the end of the trial, after a favourable summing up by the judge, the jury brought in just this verdict and she was given a five-year prison sentence. The Crown appealed against this and the Lord Chief Justice increased the sentence to nine years.

4 EVIDENCE

This includes statements made by witnesses, objects (such as the weapon used in an attack, which are usually called 'exhibits') and documents.

Evidence can be of two types: direct and CIRCUMSTANTIAL (*see* page 124). Direct evidence is where a witness actually sees a crime being committed. If this does not happen, the evidence about the crime is circumstantial.

There are certain strict rules about the presentation of evidence in court, designed to protect the accused person. Mainly they are to prevent the introduction of rumour, gossip or hearsay evidence (literally what the witness might hear someone say, but does not know to be true). In a sense a confession may be thought of as hearsay evidence, but this is allowed in court, if it is properly obtained, as it is thought that a person would hardly say anything against themselves unless it were true. In the same way a statement made by someone who is dying – and knows that they are going to die – is also admissible, because it is felt they are likely to speak the truth under those circumstances.

Opinions of witnesses are not allowed either unless they are experts, for example forensic scientists or doctors, and then only their professional opinions are accepted.

If the accused has a criminal record, this also is not admissible, nor is evidence reflecting unfavourably on the character of the prisoner, as it might influence the jury, who should make up their minds on the evidence about the crime alone. Occasionally, judges have allowed evidence relating to other crimes, for example where the prisoner may have killed more than once using the same method.

Under English law husbands and wives may not be compelled to give evidence against each other unless one accuses the other of violence against them.

REAL-LIFE EXAMPLES

● When ex-model Christine Demeter was found battered to death in her garage, near Toronto in Canada, in July 1973 her husband Peter was the obvious suspect. He had insured her life heavily, recently taken up with a girlfriend and had tried to persuade a number of people to kill his wife for money. He was charged with her murder. During the trial an escaped convict, called Laszlo Eper, was killed in a shoot-out with the police and in his room was found a paper with Peter Demeter's name on it. A friend of the convict told the police that Eper had indeed been hired, but by Christine to kill her husband! Eper and Christine however had an argument over money and the convict had killed her. But this evidence could not be presented in court because it was hearsay and Demeter was convicted of murdering his wife.

4 EVIDENCE (CIRCUMSTANTIAL)

Circumstantial evidence is the opposite of direct evidence (*see* EVI-DENCE page 123).

A good example of circumstantial evidence is a FINGERPRINT (*see* page 84). If Joe Bloggs, the well-known burglar, has left his prints all over the windowsill of Lady Moneybags' dressing room and her jewels are missing, then it is a fair guess that he took them. But supposing that in the daytime he is a window-cleaner and the day before had cleaned that very window? This illustrates the classic dilemma of circumstantial evidence. The facts are rarely in dispute: it is the inference drawn from them which can be argued about. Many judges, in addressing juries on the subject, have suggested that a circumstantial case should be like a chain. If such a chain can be built up, with each link representing a fact and reasonable deductions made from it, and it all hangs together and leads to a conclusion beyond a reasonable doubt, then it can be as convincing as direct evidence. Sometimes it is better. For a verdict based on mistaken identification, for example, can easily be an incorrect one. Oscar Slater was convicted of murder and spent 18 years in prison before being released and compensated. It was shown that the eye-witness evidence on which he was convicted was false.

Poisoning cases often rest very largely on circumstantial evidence. It must be shown that the accused had easy access to the poison which was administered or had purchased it, was in a position to administer the poison and had a sufficiently good motive for doing so. *See* also POISONS (LEGAL ASPECT) page 35.

REAL-LIFE EXAMPLES
● 19-year-old Helen Potts died at a school for young ladies in New York, one night in February, 1891, after taking a capsule given her by her boyfriend. She had died from morphine poisoning, and the capsules given her by her boyfriend, Carlyle Harris, a young medical student, to help her sleep, proved to contain morphine, but not a lethal dose. It was then discovered that Harris, who had a bad reputation with women, had secretly married Helen Potts the year before, but wouldn't make the marriage public because he was afraid his wealthy grandfather would cut him out of his will. The prosecution case was that the medical student had increased the morphine dose in one capsule to a fatal level, while leaving the others as evidence that they were harmless. The judge told the jury that circumstantial evidence is legal evidence and if the circumstances pointed to a conclusion they should consider it as if it was direct evidence. Harris was convicted of first-degree murder and executed in Sing Sing prison.

4 FOLIE A DEUX

This has been used as a defence to MURDER (*see* page 133), although it appears to have little basis in clinical psychiatry. It is referred to as communicated insanity, or a delusion or mental disorder shared by two people. It seems to have a strong sexual element. Cases are known involving two women, a man and a woman, but rarely two men.

REAL-LIFE EXAMPLES

- A good example is that of Christine and Lee Papin, two young orphan sisters who undoubtedly shared a lesbian relationship. They worked as housemaids together in Le Mans, France, in 1933 and one day for no apparent reason turned on their mistress and her daughter. They hacked and beat them to death with a knife and hammer, gouging their eyes out in the process with their bare hands. When they were separated, only one, Christine the elder and more dominant, showed unmistakable signs of madness. She later died in a mental home.
- Pauline Parker and Juliet Hulme were two intelligent teenagers in New Zealand in 1954 who developed a relationship with each other. Pauline's mother tried to break it up and so they decided to murder her. After Pauline had written a careful account of what they intended to do in her diary, they killed her with a brick wrapped in a stocking, inflicting some 45 separate injuries before the poor woman died.
- Myra Hindley (*see* also SERIAL KILLERS page 132) seemed a normal young woman until she met Ian Brady. Then, together, the two embarked on a series of bizarre and horrific crimes involving the torture and murder of young children.
- It may be difficult to distinguish between a genuine Folie à Deux and a CONSPIRACY TO MURDER (page 119) between heterosexual lovers, but Fernandez and Beck must come fairly close to Folie à Deux. There are some indications that middle-aged, balding, Raymond Fernandez was no stranger to murder and had definitely embarked on a career of fleecing gullible women even before he met 20-stone Martha Beck. But after this unlikely couple became lovers he continued to prey on women he met through Lonely Hearts Correspondence Agencies. Martha would go along as his sister when he met the women, would object strongly if he slept with any of them and killed at least two of their victims herself. They both died in the electric chair in New York in 1951.

4 HOMICIDE

This simply means the killing of one person by another. Homicide, in the laws of England and Wales, is classed as criminal or non-criminal.

Criminal homicide includes MURDER (unlawful killing with malice aforethought) *see* page 133, and MANSLAUGHTER (unlawful killing without malice aforethought) *see* page 130. In the United States there are even two degrees of murder, which must still involve malice aforethought. First-degree murder usually involves a considerable degree of premeditation. Poisoning over a long period and lying in wait to attack a victim come into this category, which in some states is punishable by death. Second-degree murder involves less premeditation and for this a sentence of imprisonment is imposed.

Non-criminal homicide also has two classes: justifiable and excusable. Justifiable homicide is where the killer is acting under authority. A public executioner is an obvious example. A policeman or soldier (in peacetime) who kills a person, would also be deemed the same provided they were acting within the guidelines laid down for them.

Excusable homicide can be either misadventure, where a person accidentally kills another – for example a motorist who kills a child who runs out from behind a parked car – or self-defence. In the latter, the person who kills must be able to show that it was necessary to save his own life or the lives of those he had a duty to protect, such as his children. Homicide during a fight is one of the commonest cases where self-defence is pleaded, but it must be demonstrated that the perpetrator took steps to avoid the conflict in the first place.

REAL-LIFE EXAMPLES
- A police patrolman in Westchester County, New York State, was shot in the head by Alex Mengel, the driver of a car the policeman had stopped on a February night in 1985. The next day a young woman, Beverly Capone, was abducted in her white Toyota car. The police did not connect the two cases until a 13-year-old girl reported that a man tried to abduct her in a white car similar to Beverly's. She picked out Mengel's photograph. Beverly's body was subsequently found and Mengel later arrested in Canada, still driving the Toyota and still in possession of the policeman's revolver. After a court appearance he was driven back to jail, handcuffed in a police car. During the journey, according to the police report, he attacked the policeman sitting next to him and tried to grab his gun. The driver pulled up, turned in his seat and shot Mengel through the head. The investigation concluded that the homicide was self-defence.

4 INFANTICIDE

The killing of unwanted children is probably as old as the human race itself. Certainly, the destruction of malformed offspring has been practised in the past by races as different as the Australian aboriginals and the Eskimos.

Population control is another reason why the disposal of infants is widely practised even today in India and China. Poor families find it difficult to provide dowries for their daughters upon marriage, and therefore will sometimes kill their baby girls. And where girls are scarce and bride prices are consequently high, parents will tend to kill their sons.

It is said that getting rid of children born out of wedlock was very common in European countries as late as the seventeenth century.

The first act making it an offence to kill an illegitimate child was passed during the reign of James I and the offence was that of MURDER (*see* page 133). For many years however it was recognised that mothers killing newborn babies during periods of depression related to child birth, or by incompetence in handling babies, could not be said to have the guilty intent or the premeditation required to substantiate the charge of murder. And, in many cases, mothers convicted of murdering their offspring were not put to death.

In 1938 the first Infanticide Act decreed that a mother who killed her own child, of under a year, would be charged with MANSLAUGHTER (*see* page 130). Only the mother can be charged with this. Anyone else who assists in the killing is charged with MURDER (*see* page 133). *See* also CHILD MURDER (page 117). And the child must in law have an independent existence, that is it must have passed from the mother's body and be shown to be alive. There must also be some proof of the mother having done deliberate harm to the baby, such as evidence of blows or strangulation or suffocation or drowning. Or it must be shown that the mother deliberately withheld proper care of the child and so caused its death.

4 INTERPOL

Bearing in mind how often police forces in this country have difficulty co-operating with each other, it is surprising that international police co-operation ever got off the ground at all. It did take a long time, however. The idea of trying to track criminals over several countries went back to the last century, but it wasn't until 1914 that the first conference on the subject was held, in Monaco. The organisation we now know today as Interpol, however, had to wait till 1946 before it received its first president and first headquarters. They were established in Paris in the Sûreté building.

Interpol is not actually an international police force. Its object is to encourage co-operation between police forces in different countries and act as a co-ordination centre for information on international criminals and criminal activities. The centre in Paris keeps in touch, by powerful radio transmitters, with 20 other centres around the world and files are kept on passport numbers, car registrations, stolen property and missing persons. Each member country, and there are over a hundred of them, has a National Central Bureau dealing with Interpol affairs, exchanging information and undertaking police work of behalf on Interpol within the compass of its own laws. And this, very often, is as far as co-operation will go. Although Scotland Yard detectives have been known to visit other countries and even interview suspects there, protocol insists that they do this by invitation of the police authority of the country concerned. Often they may have to wait on the sidelines, so to speak, while the real police work is done by the country's own police force. One of the main areas of successful Interpol involvement has been, and is, in the drug trade. And agreement has been made with the UN on extradition procedures in connection with drug offences.

REAL-LIFE EXAMPLES
● One of the most spectacular failures of international co-operation has been in connection with Ronald Biggs. While only a minor participant in the Great Train Robbery of 1963, Biggs gained international recognition by being one of the few to escape from prison and remain free. In 1974 an English journalist tracked him down to Brazil and leaked the story to the British police. Detective Chief Superintendent Jack Slipper promptly arrived in Rio de Janeiro. But Brazil had no extradition treaty with Britain and before this little matter could be sorted out Biggs' Brazilian girlfriend announced that she was pregnant. This effectively ended Slipper's visit because by Brazilian law the father of a Brazilian child cannot be deported. Biggs remained in Brazil and, as far as I know, he is there still.

4 JURY SYSTEM

People believe that if a person is convicted of a crime then he must have done it. Unfortunately, this is not always the case. The identification evidence might have been faulty, the forensic work sloppy and inaccurate or the jury – who are used in trials of more serious crimes – might have totally ignored the judge's summing up and made up their own minds. And sometimes it does not lead to justice. But this is what we pay for. Juries are *supposed* to make up their own minds. They are expected to be independent. It is their job to decide questions of fact according to the evidence, to represent the common-sense view of ordinary people and to bring in a verdict. In some states in the USA the jury may decide the sentence as well, particularly if it involves the death sentence.

Until 1967, in England and Wales, a jury decision had to be unanimous, but today majority decisions are allowed.

A jury consists of twelve people (fifteen in Scotland), who are drawn by lot. To serve on a jury a person must be a British citizen (included in the electoral roll), be between 18 and 65 years of age, and not a peer of the realm, a judge, MP, policeman, solicitor or a doctor, nor mentally ill or an ex-prisoner.

In some countries, such as South Africa, juries are not used, and in some states in the USA the prisoner can elect to dispense with a jury and be tried by a judge or judges. In Northern Ireland trials for serious offences have also taken place without a jury.

REAL-LIFE EXAMPLES
● Young Robert Hoolhouse was tried for the brutal rape and murder of an old lady, in County Durham, at Leeds Assizes in March 1938. The evidence against him was circumstantial and not very strong. His counsel, perhaps thinking the prosecution case weak, called no witnesses or evidence in defence and contented himself with making a closing statement. The judge gave the jury a broad hint, saying that the evidence was consistent with his having committed the crime, but was just as consistent with his not having committed the crime. And they needed to be satisfied beyond a reasonable doubt that he had committed the murder to bring in a verdict of guilty. The prisoner's father and mother were waiting with a taxi to take him home and most people in court expected a not-guilty verdict. However, when the jury came back, after a four-hour deliberation, their verdict was guilty. An appeal was turned down, and although 14,000 people signed a petition asking for a reprieve it too was refused. Hoolhouse was hanged in May 1938.

4 MANSLAUGHTER

The unlawful killing of a person without malice aforethought (*see* also MURDER page 133) is manslaughter, also known as culpable homicide in Scotland.

This is not such a serious crime as murder and the sentence is correspondingly less. Today, there are moves to try and make murder and manslaughter all one crime and allow the judge to fix the penalty in accordance with extenuating circumstances. At present, however, there are many types of killing which fall into the category of manslaughter. These include causing death by criminal negligence, killing where there is very strong provocation and accidentally being responsible for death while committing a crime.

There are two classes of manslaughter: voluntary and involuntary.

Voluntary manslaughter is where someone is killed during a quarrel, but there is not the intention to kill or cause injury knowing that death could result.

Involuntary manslaughter encompasses situations where death has been caused by some unlawful act which is likely to cause harm, such as dangerous driving, or criminal negligence, for example causing a baby to die by not feeding it properly.

There are also circumstances where murder can be proved, that is, the killing can be shown to be with intent, but the charge can still be reduced to manslaughter if it can be shown that the offender was acting under an abnormality of mind known as diminished responsibility (*see* also FORENSIC PSYCHIATRY page 87).

REAL-LIFE EXAMPLES
- Early in 1984, police hunting for a French student who had disappeared in the Lake District, investigated Wast Water and found a body lying in 100 feet of water. She was identified by a wedding ring and dental records as the missing wife of airline pilot Peter Hogg. He admitted killing her eight years before and dumping her body in the lake, but at his trial for murder he claimed that he had not meant to kill his wife. They had quarrelled over her long-standing love affair with another man and he had killed her accidentally. The jury accepted his plea of provocation and he was convicted only of manslaughter and jailed for four years.
- Pamela Sainsbury had suffered ten years of physical and sexual abuse from her body-builder husband. After a particularly savage beating in 1990 she waited until he was asleep then strangled him with a nylon cord tied to the bed-post. The jury convicted her of manslaughter on the grounds of diminished responsibility and the judge sentenced her to two years probation.

4 MULTIPLE MURDER (MASS AND SPREE KILLERS)

People who perpetrate multiple murders (*see* also MURDER, page 133) are classed under three headings. Although the terminology may vary somewhat from book to book they are usually known as Mass Murderers, Spree Killers and SERIAL KILLERS. (*see* page 132)

MASS MURDERERS kill many victims at one particular time and in one place. Thomas Hamilton is an example. He walked into the gym at Dunblane Primary School in Scotland on Wednesday, 13th March, 1996, and killed 16 children and their teacher.

SPREE KILLERS also tend to kill a lot of people in a short period of time, but possibly at different locations, like the Hungerford massacre.

These killers are usually male – as far as I know there have been no female mass murderers – usually white, and 30 to 40 years old. They are nearly always obsessed with firearms and these of course provide one of the most convenient means for killing a large number of people quickly. Their characteristic state of mind seems to be one of failure, either in their personal life or in their job or job prospects. And they are usually seething with resentment and revenge. The attack may be random, like shooting anybody they meet, or it may be directed against a class or group of people, like school children, teachers or fellow workers. This type of killer nearly always dies at the end of the massacre, either by committing suicide or by carrying on shooting until they themselves are shot. And it may well be that the killing orgy is simply an elaborate form of suicide.

REAL-LIFE EXAMPLES
- One of the classic examples of the spree killer was Michael Ryan. In August 1987 between 12 o'clock midday and 2.10 p.m. he shot and killed 16 people, including his own mother, and wounded another 14 in and around the little town of Hungerford, before shooting himself at 6.52 that evening. An only child, Ryan had lost his father two years before and had suffered bouts of depression over it for some time. He was unemployed and seemed to spend most of his days playing with his prized collection of firearms, but no-one knows what triggered the killing session and his final death.

FICTIONAL EXAMPLES
- Maj Sjöwall and Per Wahlöo describe the mass murder of people on a bus in *The Laughing Policeman*. But the situation is not quite what it seems...

4 MULTIPLE MURDER (SERIAL KILLERS)

Serial killings are not random murders in the same sense that MASS MURDERS AND SPREE KILLINGS (*see* page 131) are. In serial killing each victim is selected more or less carefully and often stalked before an attack is made. Then, after the murder, (*see* also MURDER, page133), there appears to be a cooling-off period before another is attempted. These periods often become shorter with a given individual the more murders that are committed. Serial killers rarely commit suicide. The majority of serial killers work alone, but Brady and Hindley (The Moors Murderers), the Australians, David and Catherine Birnie and the Lonely Hearts Killers Martha Beck and Raymond Fernandez are examples of killers who worked in pairs.

Although the quarry may be selected carefully there is usually no actual connection between murderer and victim, which makes serial killers so difficult to apprehend, but there is often a pattern to the killings, which may be done using the same weapon or weapons and in the same way. The body may sometimes be laid out in a particular manner to satisfy some inner compulsion of the killer. And personal belongings from the victim, like jewellery or underwear may be removed and kept as souvenirs or trophies. Usually, there is a high degree of gratuitous violence and often the person who was murdered seems to have been killed in a frenzy, which may have a sexual basis, since often serial killers come to find sexual release only through killing.

This applies mainly to men. Historically, women serial killers have often been poisoners who have killed their own family members, for reasons of convenience or to obtain the insurance money, like the Victorians Mary Anne Cotton, or Mrs Amelia Dyer who got rid of unwanted babies for money. Women figure less prominently in the catalogue of modern serial killers and fit the patterns less easily except perhaps for the American Aileen Wuornos who killed six men in 1989/90. Others are the nurses Beverly Allittt and Genene Jones who killed babies under their care in hospitals, and Belle Gunness, who lured a largely unknown number of elderly men to her farm in Indiana in the early years of this century and killed them for their savings.

Many male serial killers have a history of sexual and physical abuse as a child, were neglected by their parents and often showed signs of cruelty to animals and setting buildings alight. Some have sustained severe head injuries at some time in their lives. Raymond Fernandez's personality changed after a hatch fell on his head when he was a seaman, Joseph Vacher tried to commit suicide by shooting himself in the head but he did not die, Earle Nelson was hit by a streetcar and the modern Fred West nearly died from a head injury sustained when he fell from a cycle in his teens.

4 MURDER

To prove a charge of murder beyond a REASONABLE DOUBT (*see* page 137), which is the normal qualification for a guilty verdict from a jury, in the United Kingdom, a number of qualifications have to be met.

The perpetrator must not be insane, as defined by the McNaghten Rules (*see* FORENSIC PSYCHIATRY page 87), and he or she must be at least ten years old. A UK murder charge can be sustained for a murder committed outside the country, for example in colonies and protectorates, and also in ships on the high seas, aircraft and even in the Channel Tunnel – at least up to halfway along, because after that you come under French jurisdiction. Any human being can be murdered, except a child still in the womb. The infant must be deemed to be independent of the mother, in other words be breathing on its own and have its own blood circulation, even though it may still be attached by the umbilical cord. And the victim must die within a year and a day after the assault.

Probably the most important qualification is that the killing must be unlawful and with malice aforethought. Malice aforethought implies guilty intent and means that the person must have intended to kill or to cause injury which resulted in death. Even if there is no specific intention to kill, if it could be shown that the person aimed to inflict injuries knowing that death could result, this is still murder. If malice aforethought cannot be shown then the charge will be MANSLAUGHTER (*see* page 130).

REAL-LIFE EXAMPLES

- 44-year-old Gerald Smith was an overseer, working at a rail freight-liner depot near Dudley Zoo in the West Midlands. One night in January, 1975, he approached a man behaving suspiciously and was shot six times in the body. Then the gunman pressed the gun to Smith's head and pressed the trigger. The gun was empty. Smith survived for over a year, with a shattered kidney, damaged liver and perforated bowel, but then died from his wounds. The gunman could not be charged with murder because Smith had survived for more than a year and a day. But by then the assailant had been identified as Donald Neilson, the Black Panther, and convicted of four other murders and a kidnapping.
- A curious 'murder by request' case occurred in South Africa in 1961. Marthinus Roussouw confessed to killing his friend Baron Dieter von Schauroth, but said that the Baron had asked to be shot to ensure that his family would benefit from the insurance even though he had in effect committed suicide. Although there was some evidence for this, the jury didn't believe him and he was hanged.

4 POLICE PROCEDURE (FORCE STRUCTURE)

There are 43 separate police forces in England and Wales and in addition there are others such as the Railway Police, Royal Parks Police and various harbour police forces. The largest is the Metropolitan Police, which has a slightly different set of ranks to the others. The man in charge in London is called the Commissioner. Then comes the Assistant Commissioner, Deputy Assistant Commissioner and Commander. Other police forces are headed by a Chief Constable. Deputy Chief Constable comes next, followed by Assistant Chief Constable. Below this rank all forces (including the Metropolitan Police) have: Chief Superintendent, Superintendent, Chief Inspector (a rank which is in the process of being phased out), Inspector, Sergeant and Police Constable. Strictly speaking all ranks are Constables. Commonly, a police constable will address his superior as Sergeant and all the others as Sir. All forces employ numbers of civilian workers. The Metropolitan Police has 12,000 civilians to just under 29,000 police officers. The civilians normally have Civil Service ranks.

Sometimes police forces are called Constabularies, but there is little difference except that rural areas usually have Forces.

A typical force will have a headquarters. The Chief Constable will operate from there, together with his Deputy and several Assistant Chief Constables, each of whom will be responsible for a particular field, such as Traffic, Personnel and Training and so on. Support Services including Finance, Information Technology, Supplies etc, may be under civilian management with an Assistant Chief Officer in charge. The commander of the force's CID (Criminal Investigation Department), who will usually be a Chief Superintendent, may also be based at headquarters.

Each force will also have a number of territorial divisions, usually between three and seven, each under a Chief Superintendent and having its own Administration Department and CID. There will also be a series of territorial sub-divisions, each centred on one of the towns in the area, commanded by a Superintendent. And the sub-division will have a number of section stations (or police stations) commanded by an inspector or a sergeant.

The Metropolitan Police District has its headquarters at Scotland Yard. It is divided into eight territorial areas each with its own Deputy Assistant Commissioner and two Commanders.

Regional serious crime squads are set up for specific purposes. A number of forces, sometimes four or five, may combine to track down a serial killer, for example, or an organised gang operating in several cities. The search for the Railway Rapist (John Duffy) was conducted by a squad drawn from Scotland Yard, the Railway Police, Hertfordshire and Surrey forces.

4 POLICE PROCEDURE (MECHANICS OF A MURDER INVESTIGATION)

The following may vary slightly with different forces in England and Wales, but essentially the basis remains the same for all murder investigations. (*See* also SCENES OF CRIME PROCEDURES page 106.)

The person in charge of a murder investigation will usually be the head of the force's CID or his deputy, either a Detective Chief Superintendent, or Detective Superintendent. Formerly it might have been a Detective Chief Inspector, but this rank is now being phased out.

At the beginning of a murder investigation, a coach or van specially fitted out as a temporary control room, with communications, will be sited at the scene of the murder. Sometimes in cities a nearby hall or empty schoolroom might be used.

The main control room, or incident room, as it is sometimes called, will usually be at police headquarters. This has a predetermined staff, who will have been quickly transferred from other duties when the incident began. A staff officer of at least inspector rank will be in charge of it and he will have probably a sergeant who will keep a log of all pieces of evidence, statements, reports from forensic experts, etc. which come in. In addition, an exhibits officer will collate and look after all objects which will later form part of the evidence presented in court. Staff to handle clerical work will also be present and there must be adequate communications, including telephones, radio and computers.

From this control office all operations will be conducted. Squads of officers will be sent out on house-to-house investigations. Arrangements will be made to interview witnesses and suspects. All this is routine, and experienced staff will be able to get on with it on their own. This will leave the officer in charge of the murder investigation, together with his or her assistants, free to determine the broad outlines of the investigation strategy and to concentrate on the more vital pieces of evidence and the important suspects.

The officer in charge will keep the superior officers, the Chief Constable, the Deputy and the Assistant Chief Constables in the picture. If there is an Assistant Chief Constable (Crime), this officer might confer with the officer in charge at the murder site and will expect to be consulted before any major decisions are taken.

Most investigators believe that the first few days of a murder inquiry are vital, since memories of witnesses are then fresh and the perpetrator has had little time either to make a getaway or construct an alibi. Those involved are therefore prepared to work long hours, to make do with scratch meals or none at all, and often to do without sleep until the hunt has reached a satisfactory conclusion or has run out of steam.

4 POLICE PROCEDURE (ARREST AND INTERVIEW)

The rights of citizens and the powers of the police are now defined by the Police and Criminal Evidence Act (PACE) of 1984.

A person can be interviewed at a police station without being arrested and without being cautioned. But they must first be told their rights, which are that their presence is purely voluntary, they can leave at any time and have a solicitor present if they wish. Interviews will normally take place under a formalised procedure on audio tape.

If there are grounds for suspecting them of some offence they must be cautioned before interview. On 10 April, 1995, the official police caution became: 'You do not have to say anything. But it may harm your defence if you do not mention now something which you later rely on in court. Anything you do say may be given in evidence.' If the suspect is not about to be interviewed 'when questioned', may be substituted for 'now'. Before 1995 the caution was: 'You do not have to say anything unless you wish to do so, but what you say may be given in evidence.'

If the suspect cannot be interviewed immediately, or if further enquiries are necessary, the suspect can be placed in police cells. The maximum time they can be held without charge is 24 hours, unless the police are investigating a Serious Arrestable Offence (SAO), for example, MURDER (*see* also page 133), rape, armed robbery, hijacking, etc., when a superintendent can authorise a further detention of 12 hours. After 36 hours, further detention must be authorised by a magistrates' court. In certain exceptional cases, for example terrorism, detention can be extended to 96 hours.

Suspects must also be told that they are entitled to see a solicitor, at any time, unless they are being arrested for a SAO. In this case a superintendent can delay access to a solicitor for 36 hours, if there are reasonable grounds for believing that this would lead to interference with evidence, injury to other persons, alerting other suspects, or will hinder recovery of property.

A person who is arrested must again be cautioned and asked if they understand the caution. They also must be told that they have a right to legal advice in private at any time, with the exception explained above. A solicitor can also be present during interview if the arrested person wishes it and if they do not, they must be asked, for the record, why they are waiving their rights. After interview the interviewing officer will consult with the custody officer with a view to charging the suspect with an offence, or releasing them on bail to allow further enquiries to be made, or releasing them unconditionally if it is obvious that there is no case for them to answer.

4 REASONABLE DOUBT

This is the test used in nearly all criminal trials. The prosecution must prove its case beyond a reasonable doubt and the jury must have no reasonable doubts that the prisoner is guilty. This was defined by Mr Justice Darling in the Steinie Morrison murder trial (1911) as being 'such a doubt as would influence a man in his ordinary daily affairs'. In England and Wales if the jury are not satisfied beyond a reasonable doubt then they must bring in a verdict of not guilty.

In Scotland, in addition to guilty or not guilty the verdict can be 'not proven'. This seems to indicate that the jury have not gone quite as far as entertaining reasonable doubts, but feel on the other hand that the prosecution have not quite proved their case. The effect is the same as a not guilty verdict, the prisoner is allowed to go free. The famous cases of Madeleine Smith (1857) and Donald Merrett (1927) in Scotland both had not proven verdicts. Had they been tried in England they would have been lucky to have been released.

On some rare occasions a judge has asked for a verdict 'on the balance of probabilities'. An easier thing to prove than beyond a reasonable doubt. This happened in the case of Guether Podola, who shot and killed a policeman in London in 1959. He was captured after a struggle and claimed subsequently that he had lost his memory. At his trial his counsel said he couldn't present a defence because his client couldn't remember anything about the incident. Mr Justice Davies said it was up to the defence to prove their client was unfit to plead, but only up to the standard of a balance of probabilities. At the end of the trial within a trial the jury decided that Podola was fit to plead and he was eventually convicted of MURDER (*see* also page 133) and hanged.

REAL-LIFE EXAMPLES
● The standard of reasonable doubt in jury trials is held in other countries apart from the UK. Nowhere was this better illustrated than in the O.J. Simpson trial in Los Angeles, California, in 1995. The prosecution looked to have a strong case. There was much evidence that Simpson had recently threatened his ex-wife, Nicole. DNA evidence (*see* page 80) indicated that blood spots at the scene of the murder were his and blood found on one of his socks in his bedroom and on a glove outside his house seemed to have blood upon them from the murdered Nicole. And blood on the boots of Nicole's murdered friend, Ronald Goldman, also apparently showed the DNA profile of Simpson. But the defence were able to show that the methods of sample handling by the police could easily have led to contamination and erroneous results. That, together with the defence's demonstration of the racist tendencies of one of the police team, was enough to make the jury bring in a verdict of not guilty.

APPENDIX

Metric Conversion

To convert ounces to grams take the middle figure (for example
1 ounce) and read off the right-hand column (1 ounce = 28.35 grams).
To convert grams to ounces again take the middle figure (for example
2 grams) and read off the left-hand column (2 grams = 0.071 ounces).

Weight

OUNCES		GRAMS
0.035	1	28.35
0.071	2	56.699

POUNDS		KILOGRAMS
2.205	1	0.454
4.409	2	0.907

Liquid Measure

FLUID OUNCES		MILLILITRES
0.035	1	28.416
0.07	2	56.832

PINTS		LITRES
1.761	1	0.568
3.521	2	1.136

GALLONS		LITRES
0.22	1	4.544
0.44	2	9.087

Length & Distance

INCHES		CENTIMETRES
0.394	1	2.54
0.787	2	5.08

FEET		METRES
3.281	1	0.305
6.562	2	0.610

BIBLIOGRAPHY

MURDER METHODS

Cooper, Marion, and Johnson, Anthony W., *Poisonous Plants in Britain and Their Effect on Animals and Man* (H.M.S.O., 1987)
Cyriax, Oliver, *Crime – An Encyclopedia* (André Deutsch, 1993)
Farrell, Michael, *Poisons and Poisoners* (Robert Hale, 1992)
Forsyth, A., *British Poisonous Plants* (H.M.S.O., 1954)
Gaute, J.H.H., and Odell, Robin, *Murder 'Whatdunnit'* (Harrap, 1982)
Lewis, Jon E, *Means To A Kill* (Headline, 1994)
Newton, Michael, *Armed And Dangerous* (Writers Digest Books, 1990)
Stevens, Serita Deborah, with Klarner, Anne, *Deadly Doses* (Writer's Digest Books, 1990)
Wilson, Keith D., *Causes of Death* (Writer's Digest Books, 1992)

METHODS OF DETECTION

Kind, S.S., *The Scientific Investigation Of Crime* (Forensic Science Services, 1987)
Kirby, Lorne T., *DNA Fingerprinting* (Macmillan, 1990)
Knight, B., *Lawyers' Guide To Forensic Medicine* (Heinemann Medical Books, 1982)
Lane, Brian, *The Encyclopaedia Of Forensic Science* (Headline, 1992)
Marriner, B. *Forensic Clues to Murder* (Arrow Books, 1991)
Mason, J.K., *Forensic Medicine For Lawyers* (2nd Ed.) (Butterworths, 1983)
Oliver, J. S., *Forensic Toxicology* (Croom Helm, 1980)
Wingate, Anne, *Scene Of The Crime* (Writer's Digest Books, 1992)
Wilson, Colin, *Written In Blood* (Equation, 1989)

OTHER ASPECTS OF CRIME AND REVIEWS OF CRIME FICTION

Archbold, J.F., *Criminal Pleading, Evidence and Practice* (Sweet and Maxwell)
Barnard, Robert, *A Talent to Deceive: An Appreciation of Agatha Christie* (Collins, 1980)
Bintliff, Russell, *Police Procedural* (Writer's Digest Books, 1993)
Keating, H.R.F., *The Bedside Companion To Crime* (Michael O'Mara, 1989)
Lambot, Isobel, *How To Write Crime Novels* (Allison & Busby, 1992)
Melling, John Kennedy, *The Crime Writers' Practical Handbook of Technical Information* (The Crime Writers' Association, 1989)
Riley, Dick and McAllister, Pam, *The Bedside, Bathtub & Armchair Companion to Agatha Christie* (Ungar, 1979)
Symons, Julian, *Criminal Practices* (Macmillan, 1994)

INDEX

A6 murder, 95
Accidents (contrived), 4
Acetyl choline, 39
Acids, 19
- hydrochloric, 19
- sulphuric, 19
Aconitine, 37
Aconitum napellus, 37
Adam's apple, 28,65
Adenosine triphosphate (ATP), 105
Adipocere, 69
Agrippa, 36
Aird, Catherine, 15
Allitt, Nurse Beverley, 54, 132
Amanitine, 9, 36
Amanita:
- muscaria, 36
- pantherina, 36
- phalloides, 36
Amanita verna, 36
Amnesia, 12
Amyl nitrite, 48
Amytal, 57
Animals:
- attack by trained, 5
- poisonous - fish, 6
  - jelly fish, octopus, 7
  - snakes, 5, 8, 9
  - spiders, scorpions, 10
Antimony (potassium tartrate), 45
Anthony, Mark, 9
Archer-Gilligan, Amy, 81
Armstrong, Joan, 57
Arrest and interview, 136
Arsenic act, 35
Arsenic trioxide, 46
Arson, 4
Asimov, Isaac, 48
Asphyxia, 11, 21, 28, 31, 33, 44,
  65, 66, 67
- auto-erotic, 28

- crush, 11
- overlaying, 11
Atropa belladonna, 38
Atropine, 38
Augustus, Emperor, 48
Automatism, 12
Autopsy, 102
Axe, 13

Backhouse, Graham, 24, 72, 75
Bacterial poisoning, 14, 30
Ballistics, 26, 68, 70, 103
Bamber, Jeremy, 27
Barber, Susan, 59
Barbiturates, 57
Barlow, Ken, 54
Barr bodies, 73
Bartlett, Adelaide, 53
Beck, Martha, 125, 132
Bell, Mary, 87, 117
Belladonna, 38
Belushi, John, 63
Benson, Steve, 24
Benzedrine, 61
Benzodiazepenes, 56
Berkowitz, David, 26
Bianchi, Kenneth, 93
Biggs, Ronald, 128
Birmingham Six case, 77
Birnie, David and Catherine, 132
Bite-mark analysis, 68, 71, 86
Bites, animal, 71
Black Dahlia case, 118
Black Panther, 133
Black, Robert, 117
Blood group analysis, 73, 103, 110
Blood serology, 73, 110
Bloodstains, 72, 77, 110
Blue rocket, 37
Blunt instruments, 15, 92

Body temperature, 114
Booher, Vernon, 104
Borden, Lizzie, 13
Boston Strangler, 104
Botulism, 14
Brady, Ian, 20, 125, 132
Bridges, Keith, 119
British Library Newspaper Library, 2
Brittle, William, 85
Bruises, 74
Brussel, James A., 88
Buchanan, Dr Robert, 55
Bundy, Theodore (Ted), 109
Burke and Hare, 11
Burning, 16, 20
Burying (interring), 20
Bush, Edwin, 95
Bywaters, Frederick, 30

Cadaveric spasm, 75
Caesar, Julius, 9
Calhaem, Kathleen, 119
Calibre (bore), 25, 26
Calomel, 49
Camb, James, 20, 121
Camps, Dr F.E., 28, 113
Candy nose, 62
Canter, Professor David, 88
Cantharides, 52
Cantharis vesicatoria, 52
Carr, John Dickson (Carter Dickson), 17
Carr, Robert, 49
Cartridges, 25, 26, 70
Castaing, Dr Edmé, 55
Castor-oil plant, 43
Charcoal, activated, 58
Chigwell, Renée, 33
Chikatilo, Andrei, 108, 109
Childs, John, 20
Chloral hydrate, 56
Chlorthion, 60
Cholinesterase, 60

Christie, Agatha, 4, 39, 40, 44, 51, 55, 56, 67
Christie, John, 109
Christie, Susan, 122
Clark, Douglas, 109
Cleopatra, 9
Claudius, 36
Clements, Dr Robert, 55
Cobra:
   - Egyptian, Asian, 9
   - King, 9
Cocaine:
   - crack, 62
   - rock, 62
Collins, John, 91
Comparison microscope, 70, 91
Computers, 76
Conan Doyle Sir Arthur, 5
Confessions, 118
Coniine, 41
Conium maculatum, 41
Conspiracy to murder, 119, 125
Contact traces, 77
'Contre coup', 92
Cook, Robin, 47
Coppolino, Dr Carl, 39
Coroner, 120
Corpus delicti, 121
Corrosive sublimate, 49
Cotton, Mary Anne, 132
Cottonmouth, 8
Craig, Alisa, 14
Cream Dr Neil, 44
Crime kits, 78
Crime passionel, 122
Crippen, Dr Hawley Harvey, 19, 42
Crossbows, 17
Cyanosis, 11

Dahl, Roald, 30
Dahmer, Jeffrey, 64
Dailey, Janet, 62
Dalinane, 56
Daly brothers, 16

Dangerous Drugs Act, 35
Dapertuis and Hadden formula, 110
Dashwood, Samuel, 100
Deadly nightshade, 38, 42
Death cap, 36
Death:
  - cause of, 102
  - manner of, 102
  - mechanism of, 102
De Bocarme Compte Hippolyte, 58
Decomposition (putrefaction), 79
Defenestration, 18
Deighton, Len, 64
De le Pommerais, Count, 40
Demeter, Peter, 123
De Pawr, Madame, 40
Destroying angel, 36
Dexter, Colin, 22
Diabetes mellitus, 54
Diatoms, 21
Dickson, Carter, 39
Digitalis, 40
Digitalis purpurea, 40
Digitoxin, 40
Digoxin, 40
Diminished responsibility, 87
Diquat, 59
Dismemberment, 20
Disposal of the body, 19, 20
DNA profiling, 1, 71, 73, 80, 83,
  91, 103, 108, 110
Dobkin, Henry, 19, 86
Donald, Jean, 91
Doolittle, Jerome, 65
Drew, Philip Yale, 120
Drowning, 103
Druse, Roxanne, 13
Dryland, Christine, 122
Dubuisson, Pauline, 122
Duffy, John, 76, 88, 134
Dummy anthropometric. 18
Dunblane massacre, 26, 131
Duncan, Isidore, 65
Durand-Deacon, Henrietta, 86, 121
Dyer, Amelia, 132

Eastwood, Clint, 36
Ecstasy, 61
Electrocution, 22
Ellis, Peter, 22
Ellis, Ruth, 122
Embolism (air), 23, 67
Emmett-Dunne Sgt., 28
Epilepsy:
  - Epilepsy psychomotor, 12
  - Epileptic fit, 12
Ergot, 36
Erskine, Kenneth, 100
Erythroxylon cocoa, 62
Euripides, 36
Eustace, Robert, 64
Evidence, 123
Evidence, circumstantial, 124
Evidence, hearsay, 123
Evidence, witness identification,
  77, 94
Exhumation, 81
Explosives, 24

Facial reconstruction, 82
Falls, 4
FBI:
  - Behavioural Science Unit, 88
  - Serial Crime Unit, 101
  - Violent Crime Apprehension
    Programme (VICAP), 88
Fernandez, Raymond, 125, 132
Fibres, 68, 77, 78, 83, 110
Finch, Dr Bernard, 119
Fingerprints, 68, 77, 78, 83, 84, 89,
  100, 124
Finley, Eileen, 84
Firearms, 24, 25, 26, 27, 68, 70
Firth, Dr J.B., 83
Fletcher, Detective Chief Inspector,
  84
Fly agaric, 36
'Folie à deux', 125
Footprints, 100
Force Structure, 134

Ford, Arthur, 52
Forensic:
- Anthropology, 68
- Archaeology, 68
- Entomology, 79, 85
- Odontology, 68, 71, 86
- Psychiatry, 68, 87, 107, 130, 133
- Psychology, 68, 76, 87, 88
- Science, 68, 77
Forrester, C.S., 65
Foxglove, 40

Gacy, John Wayne, 53
Gerasimov, Mikhail, 82
Gibson, Gay, 20, 121
Girard, Henry, 14
Glaister, Professor John, 79, 112
Glove prints, 89
Gramoxone, 59
Gregory, Maundy, 81
Griffiths, Peter, 84
Grills, Caroline, 51
Guay, Albert, 24
Gunness, Belle, 132
Gunshot wounds, 25, 26, 27, 90

Haigh, John George, 19, 86, 121
Hair, 68, 77, 83, 91, 103, 110
Hamilton, Dr Donald, 121
Hamilton, Thomas, 131
Handguns, 26
Hanging, 28
Hanratty, James, 95
Harris, Carlyle, 55, 124
Harvey, Sarah, 79
Harvey, Dr Warren, 71
Hauptfleisch, Petrus, 97
Hauptmann, Bruno Richard, 32
Hay, Gordon, 71
Head wounds, 92
Heath, Neville, 110, 114
Heidnik, Gary, 32

Helpern, Dr Milton, 92, 113
Henbane, 42
Henry System, 84
Higgins, Patrick, 69
Hill, Dr John, 14
Hilton, David, 17
Hindley, Myra, 20, 125, 132
Hinks, Reginald, 47, 74
Hit and run, 29
Hogg, Peter, 130
Homan, Audrey Marie, 35, 46
Home Office Forensic Pathologists, 102
Homicide, 35, 96, 102, 126
Homicide Act, 12
Homicide culpable, 130
Hoolhouse Robert, 129
Hosein brothers, 20, 32
Howard, Lady Frances, 49
Hulme, Juliet, 15, 125
Hume, Donald, 18
Hungerford massacre, 131
Hurkos, Peter, 104
Hutchins, Arthur, 106
Hydrocyanic acid, 48
Hydrogen cyanide, 48
Hyocyamus niger, 42
Hyoid bone, 65
Hyoscine, 38, 42, 58, 60
Hyoscyamine, 38
Hypnosis, 93
Hypoglycaemia, 54
Hypostasis, 97

Ice bullet, 30
Identity parades, 94
Identikit, photofit, police artists, 95
Impossible methods of murder, 30
Ince, George, 94
Infanticide, 87, 120, 127
Inquest, 120
Insanity, 87
Insulin shock, 54
Interpol, 128

Ireland, Colin, 33
Isherwood, Christopher, 33

James, Robert, 8
Jeffreys, Professor Alec, 80
Jepson, Edgar, 64
Jimson weed, 42
Jones Genene, 132
Joplin, Janis, 63
Jurisprudence, medical, 68
Jury system, 129

Kaplan, Angela, 5
Karate, 28, 31
Kasper, Karl, 22
Kellerman, Harry, 47
Kellerman, Jonathan, 47
Kelly, Mary, 4
Kemper, Edmund, 67
Kersta, Lawrence G., 115
Kienzle, William, 48
Kidnapping, 32, 117
King Dot, 53
Knife wounds, 64, 67, 96
Kraft, Randy, 109
Kurten, Peter, 67

Lamson, Dr George Henry, 37
Landru, Henri, 20
Langsner, Dr Maximilian, 104
Laurens, Carolyn, 28
Le Queux, William, 24
Librium, 56
Lie detector, 101
Ligature, 28, 65
Lindbergh case, 32, 117
Lindow man, 98
Lindorfer, Friedrich, 73
Littlejohn, Professor Harvey, 69
Liver mortis, 97
Lividity, 97
Locard, Edmund, 77

Lock Ah Tam, 12
Lombrosco, Cesare, 88
Lonely Hearts Murders, 125
Loughans, Harold, 65
Lowentstein, Martha, 51
LSD, 36
Lucan, Lord, 120
Luetgart, Adolph, 19
Luminal, 57
Luminol spray, 73
Lynch, Dr Roche, 30

Macdonald, Ross, 21, 32
MacLeod, Charlotte, 58
McBain, Ed, 58
McDonald, Hugh C., 95
McDonald, Captain Jeffrey, 61, 101
McKay Muriel, 20, 32
McGinnis, Joe, 61
McGinnis, Virginia, 4
McKenny, Harry, 20
McNaghten rules, 87, 107, 133
Machine pistols, 27
Magic mushrooms, 36
Maguire family, 77
Major, Ethel, 44
Malathion, 60
Malice afterthought, 130, 133
Mamba, black, 9
Mann, Jeffrey, 5
Manslaughter, 66, 87, 107, 120 ,
    122, 126, 127, 130, 133
Markov, Georgi, 43
Marsh, Ngaio, 31, 51
Marsh's test, 45
Marshall Hall, Sir Edward, 12
Masochism, 33
Masters, David, 13
Maudsley Hospital, 12
Maw, Diana, 17
Maxwell, Susan, 117
Mengel, Alex, 126
Mercuric chloride, 49
Merrett, Donald, 90, 137

Merryfield, Louisa, 50
Metera, Lia, 41
Metric conversion, 138
Melville, Jennie, 52
Mesmer, Franz, 93
Milligan, Steven, 28
Minghella, Anthony, 22
Mogadon, 56
Molineux, Roland B., 49
Monkshood, 37
Moore, William, 92
Morgan, Samuel, 83
Morphia, 55
Morphine hydrochloride, 55
Morrison, Steinie, 137
Morse, Inspector, 22
Mortimer, Charles, 29
Motor vehicles, 4, 29, 122
Multiple personality disorder, 107
Mummification, 79, 98
Muncie, Detective Chief
  Superintendent William, 75
Murder, 108, 120, 121, 122, 125,
  126, 127, 130, 133, 136
  - bag, 78
  - child, 117, 127
  - mechanics of investigation, 135
  - multiple (mass and spree
    killers), 131
  - multiple (serial killers), 109,
    132
  - squad, 78
Muscarine, 36

Napoleon, 46
Narcotic analgesics, 55
Neave, Richard, 82
Negligence, criminal, 130
Neilson, Donald, 32, 133
Nelson, Earle, 132
Nembutal, 57
Nero, 36
Neurotoxins, 9, 10
Neutron activation analysis, 91

Ngarimu, Maria, 119
Nickell, Rachel, 118
Nickell, Stella, 48
Nicotiana tabacum, 58
Nilsen, Dennis, 20, 21
Noguchi, Thomas, 63
Not proven, 137

Oakes, Sir Henry, 15
Octavian, 9
Octopus:
  - Australian spotted, 7
  - Blue-ringed, 7
Offences Against The Person Act,
  35
Onufrejczyk, Michael, 20, 121
Operation Hart, 76
Opisthotonus, 44
Opium, 55
Oswald, Lee Harvey, 12
Overbury, Sir Thomas, 49

Paint or varnish, 99
Palm prints, 100
Palmer, Dr William, 44
Panther cap, 36
Papapaver somniferum, 55
Papin sisters, 125
Parker, Pauline, 15, 125
Parks, Ken, 12
Parton, Charlie, 56
Pathology, 68
Pavulon, 39
Pearcy, Mary, 67
Peel, Judge Joseph, 119
Peroxidase test, 73
Petiot, Dr Marcel, 19
Phorid files, 85
Piesman, Marissa, 40
Pistols, 26
Pitchfork, Colin, 80
Plato, 41
Podola, Guenther, 137

Poe, Edgar Allen, 5
Poisoning:
 - acute, 34
 - blood, 43
 - chronic, 34
Poisons:
 - fatal dose, 34
 - fungi, 36
 - herbicides, 35
 - industrial:
    antimony, 45, 46, 91
    arsenic, 35, 45, 46, 91
    carbon monoxide, 16, 47, 48,
      74, 105
    cyanide, 48, 56, 58
    mercury, 49, 51
    phosphorous, 50
    thallium, 45, 51
 - introduction to, 34
 - legal aspects of, 35, 124
 - medical:
    cantharidin, 52
    chloroform, 53
    insulin, 54
    morphine and codeine, 55, 63
    sleeping pills, 56, 57, 63
 - pesticides:
    nicotine, 35, 58
    paraquat, 35, 59
    parathion, 35, 60
 - plants
    Aconite, 37, 38
    Belladonna, 38, 58, 60
    Curare, 39, 41
    Digitalis, 40
    Hemlock, 41
    Hyoscine, 42, 58, 60
    Ricin, 34, 43
    Strychnine, 44
 - street drugs:
    amphetamine, 61, 101, 107
    cocaine, 35, 62, 63
    heroin, 35, 63
Police and Criminal Evidence Act
  (PACE), 136

Police caution, 136
Police National Computers, 76
Police procedure, 77, 106, 134,
  135, 136
Polygraph, 61, 101
Pommerencke, Heinrich, 67
Poppy, White Indian, 55
Portuguese Man-of-War, 7
Post-mortem, 102, 103, 106, 113,
  114
Potash caustic, 19
Potassium, content in eye fluid, 114
Potassium cyanide, 48
Powdered glass, 30
Precipitin test, 73
Price, Karen, 82
Prussic acid, 48
Psychic detection, 104
Psychological profiling, 88
Puckett, Andrew, 30
Pufferfish, 6
Puglistic attitude, 16

Quenzler, Julia, 95
Queripel, Michael, 100
Quicklime, 19

Rablen, Eva, 44
Radley, Sheila, 4, 29
Railway rapist, 76, 88, 134
Ransom, 32
Rattlesnake, 8
Reasonable doubt, 133, 137
Revolvers, 26
Rhyl mummy, 79
Ricinus communis, 43
Rifles, 27
Rigor mortis, 75, 79, 105
Ripper, Jack the, 67
Ripper, Yorkshire, 76, 107, 109,
  115
Robbery, Great Train, 128
Robertson, P.C., 29
Rochdale mummy, 84
Roeder, Axel, 31

Ross, Charley, 117
Rotardier, Kinglsey, 121
Rouse, Alfred, 4, 16
Roussouw, Marthinus, 133
Ruby, Jack, 12
Russell, George, 66
Ruxton, Dr Buck, 20, 112
Ryan, Michael, 131

Sainsbury, Pamela, 130
Sams, Michael, 32, 95
Sander, Dr Herman, 23
Sangret, August, 96
Saponification, 69
Sayers, Dorothy L., 23, 46
Scenes of Crime Officers
  (SOCOS), 77, 78
Scenes of Crime Procedures, 106,
  110, 135
Scheele's green, 46
Schizophrenia, 107
Scopolamine, 42
Scorpion:
  - Brown, 10
  - Common Striped, 10
  - Devil, 10
  - Giant Hairy, 10
Scorpionfish, 6
Sea Wasp, 7
Seconal, 57
Secretors, 71, 108
Semen, 108, 110
Serial killers, 132
Serin, 60
Serious Arrestable Offence (SAO),
  136
Setty, Stanley, 118
Sex crimes, 109, 110
Seymour, Henry, 64
Sharp instruments, 64, 96
Sheppard, Dr Samuel, 15
Shotgun, 25
Silverosa, George, 100
Simpson, O.J., 80, 137

Simpson, Professor Keith, 85, 96,
  105, 110, 113, 114
Sjöwall, Maj and Wahlöo, Per, 131
Skeletons, 110
Skulls, 111, 112
Slaked Lime, 19
Slater, Oscar, 124
Slater, Stephanie, 95
Slavery, 32
Sleepwalking, 12
Slipper, Detective Chief
  Superintendent Jack, 128
Smith, George, 21,75
Smith, Helen, 18
Smith, Ian, 47
Smith, Madeleine, 137
Smith, Sir Sidney, 69, 110
Smothering, 66
Socrates, 41
Sodium cyanide, 48
Sodium nitrite, 48
Sodium thiopentone, 57
Sodium thiosulphate, 48
Soneryl, 57
Spanish fly, 52
Spengler, Erwin, 19
Spider:
  - Black Widow, 9, 10
  - Brown Recluse, 10
  - Fiddleback, 10
Spinelli, Juanita, 56
Split personality, 107
Stabbing, 64, 96
Spilsbury, Sir Bernard, 21, 65, 78,
  90, 96
Stagg, Colin, 118
Stalin, Josef, 64
Stass, Professor Jean, 58
Stephenson, George, 16
Stockwell Strangler, 100
Stomach contents, 113
Stonefish, 6
Storey, Valerie, 95
Strangulation, 11, 19, 28, 65, 74
Strychnine, 9, 44

Strychnos nux vomica, 44
Sub-machine guns, 27
Succinyl choline chloride, 39
Suffocation, 66
Sutcliffe, Peter, 76, 107, 109
Swift, Patrick, 96
Syringe, Higginson, 23

Taipan, 9
Tardieu. Professor Ambroise, 40
Tartar emetic, 45
Tattooing, 90
Tetrodotoxin, 6
Thompson, Edith, 30
Thompson, Robert, 87
Thorn apple, 42
Thorne Graeme, 117
Throat cutting, 67, 96
Throttling, 65
Time of Death, 69, 97, 102, 103,
    105, 106, 113, 114
Tinning, Marybeth, 66
Todd, Sweeney, 67
Tool marks, 77, 100
Torture, 32
Toxaemia, 43
Toxicology, 68
Trajan, 37
Tregoff, Carole, 119
Trotsky, Leon, 64
Truscott, Steven, 113
Tubbs, Paul, 119
Tubocurarine, 39

Vacher, Joseph, 132

Vagal inhibition, 11, 33
Valium, 56
Venables, Jon, 87
Ventricular fibrillation, 21
Veronal, 57
Vital signs, 16
Voice prints, 115
Voice spectrograph, 115
Von Krafft-Ebing, Professor, 33
Von Schauroth, Baron Dieter, 133

Waite, Dr Arthur, 97
Walker, Neville, 33
Wallace case, 13
Walton, Charles, 64
Washerwoman's hands, 21
Wast Water case, 130
Weedol, 59
West, Fred, 132
Witchelo, Rodney, 30
Wigwam murder, 96
Wild, Deana, 4
Williams, Wayne B., 117
Wilson, Mary, 50
Windlass, Spanish, 65
Witte, Marie, 17
Wolfsbane, 37
Wuornos, Aileen, 132

Young, Graham, 45, 51

Zebrafish, 6